W9-BZN-737

East-West University

Islamic Studies

Series Editor

Ziauddin Sardar

The Islamic State

A Study
based on the Islamic Holy Constitution

Abdulrahman Abdulkadir Kurdi

Mansell Publishing Limited
London and New York

First published 1984 by Mansell Publishing Limited
(A subsidiary of the H.W. Wilson Company)
6 All Saints Street, London N1 9RL, England
950 University Avenue, Bronx, New York 10452, U.S.A.

British Library Cataloguing in Publication Data

Kurdi, Abdulrahman Abdulkadir
The Islamic state.—(Islamic studies)
1. Islam and politics
I. Title II. Series
297'.1977 BP173.7

ISBN 0-7201-1725-9

Library of Congress Cataloging in Publication Data

Kurdi, Abdulrahman Abdulkadir.
The Islamic state.

(Islamic studies)
Bibliography: p.
Includes index.
1. Islam and state. I. Title. II. Series.
JC49.K87 1984 297'.89177 84-10034
ISBN 0-7201-1725-9

Printed and bound in Great Britain by
Butler & Tanner Ltd, Frome and London

To those who have sincerely intended
to keep the word of God uppermost, and to my family,
Fāṭimah, Muḥammad, Azād, Eyād and Ajwad.
May God guide all of us to
His utmost righteousness.

Contents

Introduction 1

1 Islam and the State: A General Perspective 15

2 The Basic Foundations of the Islamic Political System 41

3 The Functions and Organization of the Islamic State 63

4 The Concepts of Peace and War in Islam 97

5 The Economy of the Islamic State: The Major Aspects 113

Conclusion 127

Appendix: The Declaration of Medina 131

Select Bibliography 139

Index, by Meg Davies 143

Introduction

Islam, usually viewed by most observers as a religion concerned only with Divine Services and personal statutes, is rather a complete system of life—a system concerned before its religious instructions with the social and governmental aspects. From its inception, the focus of Islamic ideology has been on the permanence of its polity, on its social and religious structures and on its appeal to people of all persuasions. It exhibits an inherent flexibility that encourages its followers to develop and allows reform within the system to take account of specific circumstances of time and place. Islam originally engendered a society based on such highly civilized principles as those of justice and equality for all people, giving those principles a reality that had not existed before.

The early Islamic Nation, incorporating these principles and operating in accordance with Islam's dynamic power and innate flexibility, evolved in under two centuries into a complex civilization. Social and political progress, religious enlightenment and scientific achievement came to be integral features of the Islamic revolution. The manifold advantages of Islam have become a beacon for the civilized twentieth century, inspiring scholars of all nations and faiths.

The tragic policy of Divine Right, which authorized kings and emperors to rule against the will of the people, was predominant among the world's political systems when Islam began. Thus, the early Islamic Nation, carrying out the Islamic instructions, put on the mantle of liberty and toiled actively and vigorously to emancipate neighbouring peoples who were tyrannized by the human gods of the Persian and Roman empires.

However, due to static-minded and self-deceptive administrators, the Islamic State did not remain wholly active, did not progress continuously, but experienced a gradual decline until this century. Some recent critics, on the other hand, have concluded that the major force retarding both the development and dynamism of the political, the social, the economic and the religious in present-day so-called 'Islamic states' is Islam itself—Islam which one writer claimed is 'afflicted with lethargy and superstition' (Rosenthal, 1965, p. 41).

Despite purported *objective* and *scientific* analyses, both Muslim and non-Muslim writers have based their conclusions on improper quotations from the Islamic Holy Revelation—the Qur'ān and Sunnah—and on historical grounds that are simply irrelevant. They have failed to acknowledge that Islam is far more than just a historical consequence represented by those who act officially in the name of Islam. At the outset Islam comprised influential Divine Instructions which have to be understood first and by which interpretations of historical events and consequences have to be inferred. Moreover, such writers have not considered the variables that have brought Islamic State and Nation to its present state of degeneracy; they have unfortunately ignored that Islam's potential viability has already been proved when its instructions were sincerely and comprehensively applied.

Although it is not the purpose of this book to discuss the variables that have contributed to the destruction of the Islamic State, it is important to identify the significant ones. The role of the administrators, at whose feet we have laid the major burden of the decline of the Islamic State, has already been noted. The religious scientists (ʿulamāʾ)—whose role has been significantly affected by and attributed to the decay of both the administration and society—and especially the jurists (fuqahāʾ), have participated, intentionally or not, in the decline and fall of the Islamic State. In addition, religious sectarianism, which greatly affects the powerful role of the Islamic State in maintaining order, has contributed its share. Last, but probably not least, are the waves of nationalism and capitulations to foreign powers in the Islamic State that have occurred during the last century or two.

In order to come to understand Islam as a universal and dynamic system, it is necessary first to define the Islamic System and the major requirement for its implementation; to examine Islam's basic instructions—the Holy Revelation—its content, nature and kind of Divine Instructions; and finally, to understand the role of the Muslim as a human being, as established in the Holy Revelation.

Definitions

Islam, above all, may be defined in terms of its original setting; it is a revolutionary, systematic theology and movement, directed equally against such human failings as immorality, materialism, and political and ecclesiastical tyrannies wherever and whenever such defects are seen to exist. Islam is now in quite the same position as at the time of its origin, when it countered the immorality and despotism of Arabs, Romans and Persians. The main emphasis of the Islamic System, however, is the acknowledgement of the sovereignty of God as the absolute power over all human beings, which may explain the meaning of the term 'Islam' in the Arabic language as the total and complete submission to Him alone—that is *īmān*, or faith. Īmān in Islam is not a mere feeling such as sentiment may or may not dictate. In Islamic terminology īmān is a 'system of general truths which have the effect of transforming character when they are sincerely held and vividly apprehended' (Iqbāl, 1950, p. 2).

Whenever the individual embraces Islam and possesses the capacity to understand it with those two essential provisions—sincerity and apprehension—Islam transforms that individual. Hence, the most arrogant Arab is spontaneously converted into a simple and modest personality, into a being eagerly willing to acknowledge the leadership of the son of a former slave and to care humanely for an animal which had been overloaded (Ibn-Hishām, 1955, Vol. 2, pp. 202 and 605).

Having the Holy Revelation as their guide and source of legal system for inspiration, the Muslims of the first generation came to understand the system of Islam with its religious guidance, its political and social instructions. They led armies; they dealt both militarily and politically with the most powerful and sophisticated empires of their day; they constructed a civilized state and society, even without the benefit of Islamic Law—a legal system which, according to Western scholars, did not begin to crystallize until the advent of the Abbāsid dynasty, from 750 A.D. onward (Schacht, 1950, Chapters 1 and 2). The Companions of the Prophet—the first generation of the Islamic Nation—must have possessed great jurisprudent abilities, both individually and collectively, in that they understood and extracted directly from the Holy Revelation that which subsequently became Islamic Law. Such accurate extraction was possible only because the Companions were united in faith and willing to apprehend and submit to the Holy

Revelation which closely regulated not only their personal lives but, first and foremost, the life of the body politic and the nation's social and economic concepts. In addition, the Companions were proficient in the Arab tongue, the tongue that would become the ritual language of the fatith, of Islam.

The first consideration in understanding the Holy Revelation must, therefore, be the necessity of such a faith as the basis for the Islamic Nation and State. The second requisite is the ability to assimilate, fathom and employ the Holy Revelation in conformity with its instructions and according to circumstances. The social and governmental institutions that resulted from this new revolutionary faith and which had ample time to develop in Makkah and Medina could not have been transplanted to sites or to peoples lacking the requisites for the faith's proper functioning. The same holds true in the present day: to attempt to install the Islamic system in any group of individuals necessitates that such individuals fulfill in advance those same requirements needed for that original experience, namely, faith steeped in suitable understanding.

Nature, Content and Kinds of Instructions

The Islamic Holy Revelation, the Holy Qur'ān and Sunnah, has been, and must still be considered by all Muslims and their schools of thought and law (figh) as the only constitution for the Islamic Nation and, in turn, for any proclaimed Islamic State. Therefore, the basic configuration that regulates the Muslim Nation is the 'Islamic Holy Revelation', which in political terms is known as the 'Islamic Holy Constitution', a term we shall use in this book. This belief is actually a part of the Islamic Holy Constitution's instructions advocated by the belief in the Islamic system itself. The following Qur'ānic and Sunnah verses order and direct Muslims to such a belief:

> O, you who believe, obey God, and obey the Prophet and those who are in power amongst you.
>
> Thereupon, if you have any matter of dispute refer it to God and to the Prophet [that is the Islamic Holy Constitution] if you certainly believe in God and the Last Day, that is the best deed and it is better to interpret.
>
> *The Qur'ān* 4:59

I have left you a document that, if you hold to it and follow it, you will never go astray after me—that is the Qur'ān and the Sunnah.

Abū-Dāwūd, *Manāsik*, 56;
Ibn Mājah, *Manāsik*, 84;
Al-Tirmidhī, *Manāqib*, 31;
Ibn Ḥanbal, Vol. 3, p. 26
and Vol. 4, p. 127

And whenever you differ about anything, its reference shall be to God and to Muḥammad.

Declaration of Medina, Verse 24
(*See also* Ḥamidullah, 1969, p. 44;
Ibn-Hishām, 1955, Vol. 2, p. 504;
Appendix)

Justified by these verses of the Qur'ān and Sunnah, the Islamic Holy Constitution, from the time it was first revealed to the end of this world, is, therefore, to be the only written constitution of Islam. This unprecedented, written constitution provides the foundation for the Islamic system, and for its political, social and religious aspects.

According to Muslim belief and as the Islamic Holy Constitution asserts, the Islamic Holy Constitution—i.e., the Holy Qur'ān and Sunnah—is revealed by God via the angel Gabriel to the Prophet Muḥammad in the Arabic language. The major difference between the Holy Qur'ān and the Sunnah is that the Holy Qur'ān is the actual word of God, whereas the Sunnah has been revealed by meaning and translated by the Prophet into words or action (The Holy Qur'ān 53:2–3; Al-Bukhārī, *Jihād*, 37).

Although the Islamic Holy Constitution is not a codified law; its contents may be classified in three main categories:

1. Historical background of certain prophets whose times were associated with the most significant events of the world, prophets such as Adam, Noah, Abraham, Moses, Jesus, and, of course, Muḥammad
2. Descriptive details of the unseen, such as the attributes of God, paradise and hell fire; and facts about the universal system and human nature

3. Instructions and regulations of three types:
   a. Comprehensive decisions concerning unchangeable aspects of Muslims' lives, such as marriage, divorce, and inheritance
   b. Divine Services such as *ṣalāh* (prayer) and *zakāh* (tax), which are also comprehensively decided
   c. Guidelines or sometimes merely clues concerning areas that are always susceptible to developments and changes, such as political activities

Here it should be pointed out that in these areas there may be found precise instructions in minute detail that are not subject to development and change in regard to the times.

Constitutional Law

Constitutional Law (sharīʿah) is a formal category of law, not codified, defined by the scope and provisions of the Islamic Holy Constitution. Constitutional Law accordingly is derived from the interpretation of the language of the Islamic Holy Constitution. As with most constitutions, some of the language of the Islamic Holy Constitution is so specific that it requires little interpretation. For example, the Prophet's Sunnah that assures an individual's general right of freedom does not need an exegete to explain it.

> There are three categories of people against whom I shall myself be a plaintiff on Resurrection Day. Of these three, one is he who enslaves a free man in order to sell him and to consume his price.
>
> Al-Bukhārī, *Buyūʿ*, 106

On the other hand, most of the language is general and leaves room for interpretation, as the 'due process of law' in the following verse:

> Do not kill a man whose soul has been made sacred except through the *due process of law*
>
> *The Qurʾān* 6:151

Such provisions can never be applied without first analysing them, and then making a choice between alternative interpretations in accordance with the given circumstances.

Whose responsibility is it to interpret the Islamic Holy Constitution? Who has the authority to declare Constitutional Law? In one of its verses the Islamic Holy Constitution itself proclaims, designates and refers to those who should possess such rights of interpretative responsibility. This Qur'ānic verse also recognizes the basic law of specialization in all kinds of knowledge—professionalism is an example:

> It is not the standard for the believers to respond collectively to the call to arms. But, it should have been a group from each unit devoting themselves to the study and comprehension of the legal knowledge of Islam. So, they will be a reference for their fellows when they return to them that they may be aware.
>
> *The Qur'ān* 9:122

Thus, voluntary groups from each division of the Muslim armed forces must be provided to study the Islamic Holy Constitution and furnish interpretations for each legal case. These volunteer students in the Islamic Holy Constitutional studies may consider, in fact, the basic components of the judiciary branch of the Islamic governmental order.

In regard to the responsibility of the declaration of Constitutional Law, the head of the Islamic State, depending on and aided by the Islamic State Supreme Court, is the only authority designated to declare the proper interpretation to resolve all present problems. The Islamic Holy Constitution, in a single Qur'ānic verse, has confined this responsibility:

> ... And discuss in deliberation with them [the professional Muslims] the governmental affairs, thereupon, whenever you [singular pronoun] decide then [carry out your decision and] place your confidence and trust in God ....
>
> *The Qur'ān* 3:159

This verse has established the principal governing constitutional authority in legal, social and political spheres with clear emphasis on collective—democratic—consultation procedures. It mandates the head of the Islamic State to discuss and review with the specialized governmental body every possible alternative concerning each case. Then the responsibility to choose, proclaim and carry out one of these alternatives is vested in the head of the Islamic State alone.

Accordingly, Islamic Constitutional Law (sharīʿah) is first formulated by those specialized in the study of the Islamic Holy Constitution, even during the time of the Prophet, and in conformity with the exigencies of life (Al-Bukhārī, *Maghāzī*, 30, and *Khawf*, 5). Normally on political issues, an important part of the task of interpretation of the Islamic Holy Constitution falls also upon the executive branch of the Islamic political system, which has to interpret the Islamic Holy Constitution in making daily decisions.

Thus, Constitutional Law is usually a formal category of law defined by the scope and provisions of the Islamic Holy Constitution. However, any matter treated in the Islamic Holy Constitution, even a matter of seemingly slight importance, must be resolved within the framework of Constitutional Law. Matters not treated by the Islamic Holy Constitution, no matter how important—such as the name of the Islamic System or the title of the head of that system—are usually not subject to Constitutional Law. This general standard derives from the Islamic Holy Constitution, as the following verses of the Holy Qur'ān indicate:

> O you who believe, never ask about these things [legal consequences of the facts of cases] which, if they were to be shown to you, would upset you. But if you ask about them when the Qur'ān is being revealed they will certainly be articulated. God has waived them, and God is All-Forgiving, All-Clement. A people before you asked such questions. Then they became disbelievers of the provisions [when they were announced to them].
>
> *The Qur'ān* 5:101–2

The Sunnah also stresses this matter:

> Leave me, as I do not profess a legal provision for those who lived before you and were annihilated because of their endless questions and disputes with their prophets. So if I order you to do something, do it as you can. And if I forbid you to do something, keep away from it.
>
> Al-Bukhārī, *'Itisām*, 2

> The most sinful person amongst Muslims is the one who has asked about something which was not prohibited but which was then prohibited because of his questioning.
>
> Muslim, *Faḍā'il*, 132–3

These verses from the Islamic Holy Constitution indicate clearly that matters not covered by the Islamic Holy Constitution are always liable to change according to prevailing circumstances, without hesitation and without having recourse to the precedents of any previous Islamic regime after the Prophet's death—regardless of whether the decisions concerning such matters were taken in the form of a concensus or not. More importantly, all provisions of the Islamic Holy Constitution and, in turn, of the Constitutional Law must be binding upon all Muslims, individually and collectively, who happen to live under the jurisdiction of the Islamic State. Non-Muslims who live under such jurisdiction must be excluded only from the application of the part of the Islamic Holy Constitution concerning the Divine Services. Otherwise, the Islamic Constitutional Law applies to non-Muslims as well as Muslims. Under any abnormal situation, as a matter of course, the head of the Islamic State, with the advice and consent of the Islamic Congress, has to devise temporary laws to meet such unexpected circumstances (Abū ʿUbaydah, 1933, p. 559). Also, non-Muslims who live under the Islamic territorial jurisdiction remain free to practise their own creeds in their own special temples in accordance with the provisions of the Islamic Holy Constitution. The status of non-Muslims will be explained in detail in Chapter 3.

However, Muslims must realize that their Constitutional Law has to be revised and rewritten for at least one rational and essential reason: to avoid and reconcile the almost inevitable fanatical divisions among themselves. At present, the odious divisions represented by the followers of the four orthodox schools of law ascribed to their founders have become a factor in the present-day dilemma of Muslim political and social life. Because the message of Islam was revealed to Muḥammad, the Messenger of God, Muslims must always follow not this nor that particular jurist, but the Prophet alone.

The new hermeneutic version of the Islamic Constitutional Law will certainly not reveal a great difference from the old version, especially in the portions concerning the Divine Services. However, major divergence will appear in two main categories:

1. *The style and language*. The new version of the Islamic Constitutional Law must be written in the contemporary usage of the Arabic language and style, employing all modern units of measurement, such as weights and distances.
2. *The arrangements*. There is certainly more than one acceptable

alternative for most of the legal cases treated by the Islamic Holy Constitution, due to the broad range of meaning of the text and/or the possibility of Arabic language usage. These acceptable alternatives should then be classified from the most stringent to the most lenient provisions of the Islamic Holy Constitution.

This new version and classification of the Islamic Constitutional Law will certainly guide Muslims to choose any relevant option that resolves such issues that arise, without either hesitation or having recourse to options attributed to any one of the reputable jurists of the past. The followers of these schools of law may have unintentionally attached themselves fanatically to a particular jurist and have become forgetful that the message of Islam was revealed to the Prophet Muḥammad and not to that particular jurist. Accordingly, all Muslims will be united, no one will claim his or her jurist to be right and the other wrong.

Finally, such divisions and options in the nature of the Islamic Holy Constitution indicate that the Islamic system does not conceive the human being's role in this life as merely passive and mechanistic. Islam usually formulates its regulations and instructions to give its followers more than one choice in detailed instructions that are suitable for unchangeable aspects of their lives. In areas that are subject to change and development, Islam gives outlines or clues, leaving Muslims to deduce their own procedures by thinking and acting in accordance with the given outlines and clues compatible with their exigences.

Thus, the Muslim's role in this life and in regard to the Islamic Holy Constitution is absolutely *not* passive—it is active, because Muslims are *not* ordered to follow the Islamic instruction blindly; otherwise every single aspect would be decided precisely without choice.

Scope and Methodology

It is not the intention of this book to examine every work that treats the topic of the Islamic State and its theory, but to select the most significant works, which broadly fall into three main categories:

1. Those treatises written about Islam in general and the Islamic State in particular, critical and disparaging of Islam. Generally,

such studies give readers an extrinsic knowledge of Islam, and through frequent unsubstantiated generalizations based on incomplete or ambiguously deciphered evidence usually distort the facts.

2. Those treatises authored by traditional Muslim scholars holding strong belief in the legitimacy of a certain school of jurisprudence. These individuals write of Islam either to apologize for their school's irrelevant opinions and/or to explain certain theories or facts according to their own school's particular point of view. Usually such writers are explaining the situations existing in their time or before them, justifying and documenting such conditions and arguments by selected verses of the Islamic Holy Constitution. Such writings have complicated the problems, especially for younger Muslims who found in such treatises a biased view of Islamic political history supported and justified by trivial opinions and purportedly documented by verses of the Islamic Holy Constitution. A second group of these writers are trying to reshape the example of the Prophet and his four Right-guided Caliphs and are seeking to apply some procedures and measurements of that early Islamic State. Even the famous reformers, such as, Muḥammad ʿAbduh and Rashīd Riḍā—doubt less both sincere and devoted men—could not extricate themselves from the habit of expressing the opinion of the four well-known schools of jurisprudence and of tracing earlier events. At the same time all these reformers assert that reform must be derived directly from the Islamic Holy Constitution.
3. Those treatises written by semi-revolutionary thinkers, including the works of the two renowned writers Al-Mawdūdī and Muḥammad Asad, who touch upon the theory of the Islamic State and have fairly recently written about it as they conceive it. Regardless of their revolutionary ideas they follow closely the direction of traditional thoughts. Moreover, they have emphasized not establishing new legislation or law before consulting these schools which have become spontaneously as sacred as the Islamic Holy Constitution. At any rate, the diversity among these writers has assuredly directed the attention to the need to derive Islamic political thought from its original source alone.

Before examining the specific procedure, some overall aspects of this research process should be mentioned. First, specific references to the

Islamic Holy Constitution include the Holy Qur'ān; the Glorified Sunnah, which consists of the record of the Prophet's sayings, acts, deeds and the record of acts and deeds of the Companions that the Prophet approved explicitly or by silence; and also the Companions' sayings, acts and deeds which would have been impossible for them to say or do without explicit direction from the Prophet, mostly introduced without reference to the Prophet because it is clear the Companions would not so say or do unless they had been instructed.

Secondly, logical analogy (qiyās) will never be considered as a source of the Islamic legislations, but only as a tool to enlarge the scopes and the dimensions of the Islamic Law. Thus, Islamic legislations must always depend upon the Islamic Holy Constitution as a sole and original source only. Logical analogy, accordingly, can be used to extend the dimension of this primary source.

Moreover, the Islamic historical record, especially that concerned with the Prophet's period, will be weighed and considered as an example, particularly when the historians confirm the event. However when any given situation in which the Islamic Holy Constitution declines to instruct the believers and deliberately has left it up to them to decide for themselves independently, a solution will be suggested in conformity with the general basis of the Islamic system as perceived by the author, far from polemic argumentation in most cases. It should be emphasized, however, that any such suggestion or decision must not be considered final, but always subject to change according to the prevailing circumstances.

Finally, throughout this work an attempt has been made to reconstruct theoretically an Islamic State in accordance with the Islamic Holy Constitution's instructions, to perceive how far the Islamic concept of the state is related to the idea of statehood in modern times.

The basic method and structure is designed to provide a general framework to analyse the major forces and issues affecting the Islamic political system. In order to do so it is important to examine that special portion of the Islamic Holy Constitution relating to the main topic of investigation. The scientific method employed for analysing and treating the texts will be the Prophet's method prescribed to one of his Companions, Muʿādh, who at the time was sent to Yemen as a governor of that province. The Prophet states:

> O, Muʿādh, which law are you going to apply in your judging? Muʿādh said: 'I will apply the Qur'ānic laws'. The Prophet then said,

'What are you going to do if you do not find such law in the Qur'ān?' He said, 'I will apply the Prophet's Sunnah.' The Prophet said, 'If you do not find such a law in the Sunnah?' He said: 'I will try my utmost and judge accordingly.' The Prophet pleasantly put his hand on Muʿādh's chest and said, 'Praise be to God Who directs the messenger of the Messenger of God to the correct path which satisfies God and His Prophet'.

Ibn Ḥanbal, Vol. 5, 230, 236, 242

The guideline above is the significant major and basic method followed; however, the exegetical method for the interpretation of the texts of the Islamic Holy Constitution will be one of the most acceptable methods among the Islamic exegetes, summed up as follows:

1. A verse of the Islamic Holy Constitution can be a self-explanatory verse, a type of verse that usually uses precise Arabic terms.
2. A verse can be explained, elaborated, restricted or abrogated by another verse or verses.
3. A verse may represent an answer or judgement for certain questions or events arising at the time of revelation. Knowing the cause or purpose of the revelation in such verses gives a broad vision for their interpretation.
4. In all situations, the Arabic lexical meaning and the common Arabic usage of term(s) included in the verse give a precise exegesis.

As it is impossible to translate the Islamic Holy Constitution verbatim or literally into English, the verses of the Holy Qur'ān and Sunnah quoted in this work are first worked out to their final Arabic meaning before being translated into English.

The terms *Sunnah* and *Ḥadīth* will be used interchangeably unless otherwise indicated. The records of the Sunnah compiled by Al-Bukhārī, Muslim, Al-Tirmidhī, Ibn Mājah, Al-Nasā'i, Al-Dārimī, Abū-Dāwūd, Ibn Ḥanbal, and Imām Mālik will be referred to in accordance with the *Concordance et Indices de la Tradition Musulmane* (Wensnick, 1965). Regarding the State organizations, the model of the Prophet and that of the four Right-guided Caliphs will be considered as the prime examples to be developed in accordance to the need and prevailing circumstances.

At any rate, this book is solely confined to political aspects of the

Islamic System. Social organizations and religious activities will be referred to only as they relate to the issues under investigation. However, a referential background is presented in some detail, including the basic elements of the original Islamic polity, such as its concepts of equality and justice, which affected to a large degree the viability of the system. Also, the aspects of peace, war and economy in the Islamic system are deemed to be interrelated to the political concept of Islam. Thus, the major rules concerning such aspects are provided.

Finally, in order to assure the objectivity of the research, especially in analysing the content of the Islamic Holy Constitution, all terms that are used to refer to the Islamic Holy Constitution specifically are carefully defined according to their lexical meaning and to their usage in the early Islamic period. Otherwise, all terms that have been invented by the jurists (fuqahā') are avoided and other modern terms are used to make the subject more understandable. A high degree of certainty in understanding the texts and terms is aimed for so that the final decision will be consistent with the spirit of Islam.

1

Islam and the State: A General Perspective

Students of Islamic studies have generally assumed that the Islamic Holy Constitution does not confer a positive or even imply any information about the Islamic polity and its social and political organizations. In effect, the Declaration of Medina which announced to the world the birth and establishment of the first Islamic State indicates the official promulgation of the Islamic State, headed by Prophet Muḥammad as the temporal and spiritual leader of that first nation of Islam (*see* Appendix, verses 23, 36, 42).

The Declaration of Medina has also proclaimed that the Islamic polity would certainly function in accordance with the Islamic Holy Constitution and its Constitutional Law provisions. Accordingly Muslims and non-Muslims of that first state of Islam would abide by the Islamic Holy Constitution, especially in regard to the social and political instructions (*see* Appendix, verses 23, 42).

However, in discussing the Islamic political system, Muslim thinkers have written numerous tracts in which they have tried to justify Abū Bakr's succession after the Prophet's death. Although it was logically necessary to fill the vacant temporal position of the Prophet, those Muslim thinkers, and specifically Al-Bāqillānī, have gone so far as to quote the Islamic Holy Constitution to support their remarkable deductions (Al-Bāqillānī, 1947, pp. 164, 239; Ibish, 1966, pp. 29–145).

At any rate, before preparing the theoretical example for the Islamic State's political organizations as it is conceived from the Islamic Holy Constitution, it is necessary to introduce a general perspective of the Islamic Holy Constitution's text that deals, more or less, with the main topic of investigation. The major concern, therefore, in this chapter and the following one will be to provide a general foundation and perspective for the political issues concerning Islamic political organizations.

The first of the three sections in this chapter deals briefly with the ancient political systems referred to in the Islamic Holy Constitution. The second section treats one of the most polemical topics—the alleged contrast between reason and religion, especially in the Islamic system. Moreover, ethics and moral values are more or less bound together by the criterion of reason serving to differentiate moral from immoral acts. The Islamic framework for inquiries into these matters is reviewed briefly. And, finally, the third section presents the Islamic attitude toward the issue of sovereignty and examines to whom the Islamic Holy Constitution bestowed that most profound Will.

Ruling Systems

It is impressive that about eighty percent of the Qur'ānic verses focus on the nations of the world before the advent of Islam. On many occasions the Sunnah either comments in detail on these historical incidents or explains their causes as historical phenomena. However, the predominant concern of the Qur'ānic review of these parables is to survey the real purpose behind the decline and fall of those civilized nations. The Holy Qur'ān concentrates mainly on how those nations, which had cherished prosperity and wealth, behaved in response to God's messages.

The phenomena the Qur'ān repeatedly illustrates may be summed up in three points. The first is that the elite of those nations almost always rejected the messages of God. The second point is that their rejection was not because they assumed these messages to be untrue, but because the consequences of following them usually necessitated reform on the basis of equality, justice and freedom for all honourable creatures of God. Assuredly, the application of these principles would upset the prevailing systems of those nations, systems dominated mainly by men of means. Any renovation based on such principles would certainly threaten the power of the elite who in turn would lose their ability to manipulate their societies according to their own personal interests. The third point is that the first followers of God's messages were invariably victims of tyranny who had been seeking salvation from the despotism imposed on them. The historical parables always illustrate the severe punishment of those who reject the light of God.

The frequent projections of historical senses in the Holy Qur'ān are not merely to add eloquence or diversity of style, but are primarily to emphasize certain aspects that should have received greater attention from Muslims in their socio-political behaviour. However, the governmental systems discussed in the Islamic Holy Constitution, as examples of justice or injustice, comprise three distinct types: the Monarchical System (mulk); the Junta System (malā'); and the Tyrannical System (ṭāghūt). Only a verse or two from the Islamic Holy Constitution addressing each system in question will be quoted. The entire system and its overall functioning is too broad a topic to consider here.

THE MONARCHICAL SYSTEM—MULK

The Monarchical System is illustrated in the Islamic Holy Constitution in many diverse styles and patterns. The three most outstanding examples are the kingdoms of Ṭālūt (Saul), Dāwūd (David), and Sulaymān (Solomon).

The Kingdom of Ṭālūt—Saul

After the death of the Prophet Moses, the temporal leaders of the Israelite people ruled jointly, much like a council. However they were deemed weak by their enemies and felt that their leadership should be united, especially if they were to defend themselves. The following Qur'ānic verses explain how the Israelites chose a ruler:

> Have you considered the council of the sons of Israel after Moses, when they said to one of their prophets, 'Dispatch a king for us. We will fight for the sake of God'? He said, 'Might you, if fighting were forced on you, refrain from fighting?' They said, 'Why should we cease to fight for the sake of God, when we with our children have been expelled from our habitations?' Yet when fighting was forced upon them they fled, save for a few. And God is Omniscient concerning the iniquitous.
>
> *The Qur'ān* 2:246

> Thereupon their Prophet told them, 'Verily God has dispatched for you Ṭālūt as a king'. They said, 'How can he be king over us while we are more fitted for the kingship? Besides, he has never been given an abundance of wealth.' He said, 'Surely God has chosen him over you and has broadly increased his knowledge and the strength of his body. And God gives His kingdom to whom He will, and God is Liberal and Omniscient.'
>
> *The Qur'ān* 2:247

The individual quest for power among the ruling elite prevented the election of only one man as king from among themselves. Eventually recognizing that the nomination of their king would come directly from God, they appealed to their current prophet to designate a king to lead them in the fight for God's cause. However, as they felt the power slip from their hands, they rejected God's nominee, claiming that he did not satisfy their criterion for wealth. When God asserted that He had chosen Saul, who suited His own standard of wisdom and health, they would have to obey Him.

The two verses also indicate a resolution of one of the most controversial topics in Islamic politics. Political theorists have insisted on the necessity of leadership in the Islamic Nation, but they have disagreed as to whether the leadership is demanded by reason or by revelation (Al-Māwardī, 1966, pp. 4–7). Thus the two verses assert that the necessity of individual leadership, especially in the case of war, is demanded by reason; an example is when the Israelistes asked for a leader. The election of a leader was also approved by revelation—God Himself appointed Saul their first king after the death of their spiritual and temporal leader, the Prophet Moses. It seems that the rejection of the Israelite king appointed by God is one of the reasons God did not appoint a successor to the Prophet of Islam. Instead He left the believers to choose their own leader, lest the nominee otherwise be rejected.

The Kingdom of Dāwud—David—and of his son Sulaymān—Solomon

After his appointment, King Saul led the Israelites to fight Jālūt (Goliath), a man of extraordinary strength. Saul proclaimed that whoever killed Goliath would become a king of the Israelites. The following verse explains the rest of this parable:

> Thereupon they routed them, as God ordained; and David killed Goliath. And God gave him the Kingship and wisdom and taught him what He would.
>
> *The Qur'ān* 2:251

The Prophet Solomon was overly ambitious. When he inherited his father's kingdom he prayed to God:

> He said, 'My God, forgive me and bequeath to me a Kingship which may not befall anyone after me. For You are the Grantor.'
>
> *The Qur'ān* 38:35

The four succeeding verses enumerate what Solomon was given. The kingdoms of the Prophet David and of his son, the Prophet Solomon, appear at length in the Islamic Holy Constitution. Many verses describe the kingdoms and their appropriate rulers in terms of the justice and equality which distinguished their kingdoms by God's blessing. Both kings are described as thankful and humble.

THE JUNTA SYSTEM—MALĀ'

The term *malā'* is used in the Islamic Holy Constitution in accordance with both its lexical meaning and common Arabic usage. The term denotes:

1. The elite people in general
2. The members of a council who associate with a certain leader
3. The members of a council or committee who rule collectively
4. Any group of people
5. Consultation (Tashāwur)

See Ibn Manẓūr, n.d., s.v. *Malā'*. This study confines itself mainly to that indicated in number three above. Two examples serve to represent the *malā'* at the time of the Prophet Nūḥ (Noah) and the Prophet Shuʿayb.

The parables of Noah and Shuʿayb are usually presented in the Islamic Holy Constitution as dialogues between the prophet and his people's leaders, the council.

The Prophet Noah and his Malā'

> Surely, we sent Noah to his nation and he said, 'O my fellows, worship God! You have no other god except Him. Verily I fear for you the chastisement of the dreadful day.' Said the council of his nation: 'We see only that you are obviously astray'. He said, 'My fellows, I am not being deluded, but assuredly I am a Prophet from God, the Master of all beings'.
>
> *The Qur'ān* 7:59–61

Noah's story appears in the Islamic Holy Constitution in various styles, each emphasizing a different aspect. Usually Noah spoke to all his fellow citizens, but the response always came from the ruling council of the leaders of his nation who, representing power and the prevailing system, in turn manipulated the society according to their own interests. In the above verse Noah called for the unity of godhood and asked his people to worship God alone. The junta immediately answered by accusing him of the delusion of prophethood.

The Prophet Shuʿayb and his Malāʾ

The parable of the Prophet Shuʿayb resembles that of the Prophet Noah. He was sent to the people of Madyan (Midian), being one of them. They were merchants and traders who used their weights and measures falsely in purchasing people's goods in order to make great profits. The following verses illustrate their situation.

> To the people of Midian We sent their brother Shuʿayb. He said, 'O my fellows, worship God, you have no other god but Him. There has now come to you a clear sign from your God. So fill up justly your weights and measures and do not appraise unjustly the people's goods; do not corrupt the earth after it has been set right; that is best for you if you are believers.'
>
> *The Qurʾān* 7:85

> Said the Council of his nation who was haughty, 'We will expel you from our town, O Shuʿayb, and those who believe with you too, unless you return to our creed.' He said, 'What? Even though we were grudged?'
>
> *The Qurʾān* 7:88

As his junta seemed so powerful the Prophet Shuʿayb was in the worst predicament. The council threatened him and those who believed with him, either to return to the council's belief or to face expulsion from their town.

These examples illustrate the idea of the junta system, or of a powerful council governing the affairs of the city and its people. According to the Islamic Holy Constitution, the malāʾ, or junta, usually consisted of the men who defended the city against outside attack and also kept order within. This system was common in the ancient world. Prior to Islam, Makkah was ruled by a council representing the clans of a large tribe. This council usually enforced the law, defended and governed the city. Normally every citizen abided by its decisions. However, this type of ruling class served its own interests first and the general welfare second.

THE TYRANNICAL SYSTEM—ṬĀGHŪT

Two tyrannies described in the Islamic Holy Constitution exemplify systems based on absolute dictatorship that were devoid of any justice and/or equality. The systems were modeled on the pattern of a kingdom, but their leaders, gradually corrupted by power, assumed the status of gods. The first example is Al-Namrūd ibn Kanʿān (Nimrod), a king at the time of the Prophet ʾIbrāhīm (Abraham). The Islamic Holy Constitution does not name him; his name is taken from Islamic history (Al-Ṭabarī, 1968, Vol. 3, pp. 23–7). He is called 'the one who disputed with Abraham concerning his God', as the following verse of the Holy Qurʾān illustrates:

> Have you considered him who disputed with Abraham concerning his God, despite God's bestowal of the kingship over him? Abraham said, 'My God is He who animates and terminates'. He said, 'I too animate and terminate'. Abraham said, 'Surely God has designed the sun to rise from the east; would you cause it to rise from the west?' Thus perplexed was he who disbelieved. And God never guides iniquitous people.
>
> *The Qurʾān* 2:258

The second example is that of the Pharaoh of Egypt who was a king at the time of the Prophet Moses. Two verses of the Holy Qurʾān serve to explain his situation.

> So when Moses came to them with our obvious signs and tokens they said, 'This is nothing but forged sorcery. We have never heard of this from our ancient fathers.' Thereupon Moses said, 'My God knows who came with guidance from Him, and who shall have the blissful end. Surely, he never redeems the iniquitous.' Thereupon Pharaoh said, 'O Council, I never knew you had a god except me. Kindle me, Haman, a fire upon the clay that I may launch myself up to Moses's God. For I surmise that he is one of the liars.'
>
> *The Qurʾān* 28: 36–8

> 'Thus, he [the Pharaoh] rejected the intelligence and insight of his nation so that they would obey only him. They were profligate people'.
>
> *The Qurʾān* 43: 54

In the first example, King Nimrod is mentioned only once in the second chapter of the Holy Qur'ān. The story indicates that while Abraham was conveying the message of God to him, Nimrod was arguing with Abraham about his own supreme power and comparing his ability to that of God. Attempting to demonstrate Nimrod's limited power, Abraham told him that God has the power to animate and terminate. Nimrod immediately claimed the same power. To prove his claim to Abraham, Nimrod called for two prisoners sentenced to death and ordered his servant to kill one of them and give pardon to the other. Abraham assumed that Nimrod was truthful in his example and expanded the argument to include feats impossible for a human to perform. He asked Nimrod to change the course of the sun making it rise in the west. Nimrod surrendered and was astonished with his limited power and could no longer challenge Abraham (Al-Ṭabarī, 1968, Vol 3, pp. 23–7).

The second example is the Pharaoh of Egypt who ruled at the time of the Prophet Moses. Many details are given by the Islamic Holy Constitution about this Pharaoh who exploited the Egyptians by claiming the status of godhood. The story of the challenge of the Prophet Moses described and emphasized Pharaoh's tyrannical acts against the Egyptians and the Israelites. It seems that the idea of proclaiming the status of godhood (associated with the ruling family in Egypt) was not necessarily initiated before the Prophet Moses's time. According to the Islamic Holy Constitution, this Pharaoh may be the first of the Egyptian ruling family to apply the notion of deity to himself, which he did, while the Prophet Moses was calling him to Islam, to the submission to God (*The Qur'ān* 7:103–28; 26–11; 68:28; 3:48).

These two examples represent not merely ordinarily powerful kings, but two dictators so intoxicated by an almost absolute power that they were incited to proclaim themselves gods. Consequently, they subdued their nations to carry out their will by force.

Finally, before analysing these ruling systems, it should be pointed out that the Islamic Holy Constitution teaches Muslims that power should always be utilized to serve human beings, not to subdue them. One of the main objectives of such teaching is to retain the humanity of mankind by spreading justice, equality and freedom among them.

REVIEW AND COMMENT

To analyse these three ruling systems, one should first possess a clear understanding of the terms *malik*, *mulk*, *malā'* and *khalīfah*, which all refer to the power exercised over people.

Malik and mulk, respectively, denote the English terms 'king' and 'kingship', and have been used by the Holy Qur'ān to describe both the prophets and tyrants in regard to their positions as rulers. The Qur'ānic use of these two terms is generally equivalent to Arabic lexical use and to common Arabic usage. The common Arabic application of the word 'malik', denoting a person who holds power over a certain nation, is synonymous with the term 'amīr', meaning one to whom people pay homage and obey. However, in the sense of power, malik has a much broader meaning than amīr. So every malik is an amīr, but not vice-versa. The term 'mulk' usually symbolizes the power that the malik exercises over his subjects. The lexical meaning of malik indicates the implications of absolute power (Ibn Manẓūr, n.d., s.v., *malak*). The Islamic Holy Constitution does not emphasize any significant difference in the use of the terms 'malik' or of 'mulk' to denote the role of the prophets or tyrants.

The term 'malā'' is discussed earlier in this chapter, in the section headed 'The Junta System'.

Khalīfah was used twice in the Holy Qur'ān (2:30; 38:26) to describe both the Prophet Adam and the Prophet David. In both verses the term 'khalīfah' denotes the one responsible for keeping order and carrying out the laws. Both prophets Adam and David were, of course, implementing the law of God.

Traditionally khalīfah is translated into English by both Muslim and non-Muslim writers as an equivalent of the term 'vice-gerent'. Actually there is no relation between the two terms, especially considering that most writers assume that 'vice-gerent' refers to one holding power through the delegation of God (Rosenthal, 1962, pp. 21–60). Usually writers use *khalīfah* to mean God's deputy on earth. However, the original root of the term is the verb *khalafa*, which generally means in both its common Arabic usage and lexical meaning, 'coming after the other', i.e., 'to succeed'. The actual meaning of the verb, however, is determined by the preposition that follows it. The verb is most commonly followed by the proposition 'in' (في), or 'on' (على), but each of the cases denotes a substantially different meaning. For instance, Arabs say, (السيد « أ » خلف السيد « ب » في أهله (Mr A succeeds [khalafa] Mr B *in* his household), by which they mean that Mr A. is substituting for Mr B in managing the affairs of his house, as his deputy according to Mr B's requests. But when they say, السيد « أ » خلف السيد « ب » على أهله (Mr A succeeds Mr B *on* his household), they mean that Mr A has married Mr B's divorced wife and has taken over his place without Mr B's permission, although the permission of the wife is understood (Ibn Manẓūr, n.d., s.v. *khalafa*; Al-Muwaṭṭā', *Aqḍiyah*, 22; Al-Bukhārī, *Jihād*, 38). In the two Qur'anic verses (2:30; 38:26) that use the term 'khalīfah' (Caliph) the word is followed by the preposition 'in'. However, if the two verses had used the preposition 'on' (Caliph on the earth instead of Caliph in the earth), it would indicate that the khalīfah in question is meant to be the vicegerent of God who has taken over the responsibility without the permission of those whom he rules. But the use of the preposition 'in' indicates that the khalīfah is the one who is deputized by his people, with their obvious or implicit consent, to carry out or enforce the law.

Another issue involves the precise usage of the verb 'khalafa', which in the Holy Qur'ān is followed by the preposition 'in' to show the actual application of the meaning. The story relates that when Moses went to fulfill the appointment of God, he commanded his brother Aaron to serve as a deputy until he should return, saying 'Ukhlufni fi qawmi—Deputize me in my nation' *The Qur'ān* (7:142). Aaron could never command the same degree of obedience as could Moses. When some of the Israelites took advantage of Moses's absence and disobeyed his instructions by worshiping the Golden Calf, they insisted on such a practice even after Aaron advised them to return to Moses's revealed instructions, saying that they would not give up their worship of the Golden Calf until Moses returned. They realized that this matter was so significant that the decision of Moses's deputy would not suffice. Since Aaron was deputized by Moses and not by them, his succession was not completely valid. Obviously, had Aaron been the original leader he would not have hesitated to force those who so deviated from the basic belief back into obedience, even if it required using his ultimate force.

In conclusion, the term 'khalīfah' as used in the Islamic Holy Constitution denotes a deputy who takes care of and manages the affairs of the original. The original, accordingly, is the group of ruled people who have authorized the deputy to carry out the law and keep order.

The main ideas behind the ruling systems mentioned in the Islamic Holy Constitution may be summed up in the following points.

1. To provide an historical heritage and tradition of world history, based on accurate prescription as a common heritage of the Islamic Nation.
2. To draw certain general provisions for the Islamic government which are the most significant and desirable output of any system, i.e., to provide an accurate standard of equality, justice and freedom.
3. To avoid certain undesirable behaviour on the part of the Islamic Nation, which was one of the main reasons for the destruction of nations.
4. To provide a general rule for the Islamic Nation to choose the most appropriate government based on the consultation of the believers and to provide them whatever is suitable for the dignified creation of God.

As these examples indicate, the name of the system and the way it is organized is not necessarily as important as its outcome in providing justice and equality for the ruled. In fact this idea is the main one behind all messages of God, after the acknowledgement of His oneness.

The Islamic Holy Constitution and Reason

> Read: 'By the name of your God Who created. [He Who] created man out of a clot.' Read: 'And your God is the most generous. He Who taught [writing] with the pen; taught man that which he does not know.'
>
> *The Qurʾān* 96:1–5

Many researchers of Islamic thought have erroneously concluded that in Islam, the problem of revelation versus reason presents itself chiefly in the form of contrast between Divine Law and human reason (Rosenthal, 1962, p. 16). More accurately, had there ever been any contrast between Divine Law and human reason it would have been impossible for the Islamic Holy Constitution to commence with the word 'read'. Unrestricted reading provides an essential access to awareness and is, in turn, a *modus operandi* for human reason to awaken and develop in order to comprehend the intricacies of life. Reading, introduced in the Islamic Holy Constitution as an injunction, indicates that human reason must vehemently avoid following any instruction which does not feature the criterion of reason. To prevent man from blindly accepting any and all instructions, God crowned reading with His own name: 'by the name of God Who creates' and 'Who teaches man knowledge which he does not know'.

Two other injunctions can be extracted from the verses above, in which the order to read has been repeated twice. The order does not refer merely to the ability to read; it definitely means, as its meaning in Arabic and in English indicates, to apprehend, to scrutinize, and to contemplate what has been read. The second injunction is that not all information transmitted to human reason should be considered salient truths or facts. For this reason, too, it may be concluded that reading has to be crowned by the name of God to prevent human reason from any deviation or deviousness of rational and empirical investigations.

According to the Islamic Holy Constitution, fact can derive only from empirical deduction or sound induction. However, the absolute fact or ultimate reality, which may lead man to know objectively the basis and connections of all universal systems, still cannot be understood unless man knows the groundwork or the laws of every single system, including that of the metabolism of the human body. These groups of single laws or facts may then be arranged into a certain systematic set of inter-relationships that will eventually define for man that ultimate reality. Facts, or sometimes theories, that man might discover every day could be likened to a small acorn in a huge oak tree or even to a part of that acorn itself. Most of the time man discerns no association or relationship between facts; he thus immediately assumes that such facts are either isolated from one another or contradictory to one another. What has happened is that man's discovery or perception of facts is not in accord with their original arrangement in the great oak or circle of knowledge. Discrepancies invite man to render false judgements. Because of these discrepancies, the Islamic Holy Constitution directs man's attention to the universal manifestations and explains significant portions of historical events and parables through logic, analogy and empirical deductive and sound inductive methods. Such examples are designed to allow the capacity of human reason to evolve as a receptor of knowledge and to develop its ability to differentiate between facts and counterfeit propaganda (*The Qurʾān* 23:71, 21:22, 6:74–9, 38:21–6, 27:20–7. Al-Bukhārī, *Farḍ Al-Kumus*, 19; *Tafsīr* 63: 1–3, 24:6. *Kurdī*, 1974, pp. 18–30).

On many occasions the Islamic Holy Constitution uses the verb *ʿaqala* (to reason) in order to direct man's attention to the many diverse manifestations of the universe, such as day, night, earth, sky, wind, clouds or stars. Accordingly, nothing goes unseen in the universal system; everything happens according to delicate laws clearly manifested by the One who keeps His eyes open. Direction for man to utilize his mind and contemplate such phenomena has repeatedly appeared in the Islamic Holy Constitution. The following three Qurʾānic verses demonstrate these directions:

> How do you order the people to piety and forget yourself while you are reciting the Book? Do not rationalize.
>
> *The Qurʾān* 2:44

> Surely, in the creation of the heavens and the earth and in the alternations of the day and the night, and in the vessel that runs on the sea for people's welfare, and in the water God has sent down from heaven, therewith reviving the earth after it has died and scattering within it crawling creatures of all types, and in regulating the winds and clouds subjugated between the heavens and earth, surely these are signs for people of rationality or reason.
>
> *The Qurʾān* 2:164

> Say, had God willed, I would not recite it to you, and He would prevent you from knowing it. I have remained amongst you for a long time before it [was revealed to me]. Will you be reasonable? [Or will you rationalize?].
>
> *The Qurʾān* 10:16

These quotations from the Islamic Holy Constitution, like many other verses, direct man to use his reason and not to judge haphazardly according to what he has read or has heard. Reason must evolve and develop freely in accurate and sound ways, so that it may serve to discover facts and, in turn, to distinguish between truth and falsity (*The Qurʾān* 6:73–83).

The most significant issue to be raised concerning the contrast between Divine Law and human reason is where the contradiction appears between the two components. Etiene Gilson concludes that there are 'two distinct orders of assent—religious faith and rational knowledge. I know by reason that something is true because *I see* it is true: but I believe that something is true because *God has said it*' (Gilson, 1939, pp. 72ff). This kind of paradoxical analysis might well apply in light of the way the Church functioned in mediaeval Europe. Then the Church was the only source of law; it forcibly determined the acceptance of reason and human conduct allegedly in the name of God. The priests, in co-operation with the papacy, issued laws to prescribe and proscribe legal cases as well as to govern man's cultural and social life to maintain the status quo, such laws usually serving the dominant rulers and interests. Of course, most of the laws issued by the Church were not accepted on the basis of any level of reason. In contrast, Islam has always emphasized the liberation of the human mind and man's free choice to accept the Islamic Holy Constitution with his comprehensive understanding and satisfaction based on rational inquiry. The Islamic Holy Constitution speaks of this intent in the following verse:

> No compulsion must exist in religion. Evidently rectitude has been distinguished from caprice.
>
> *The Qurʾān* 2:256

Two major principles may be derived from the above verse: first, the human mind must be free from any compulsive belief or prejudice; second, Islam must be introduced to human beings in a decent and clear manner, without forcible manipulation or indirect instructions, because the Islamic faith (īmān) can be totally proved by rational thought. Otherwise, such is not faith but a sort of sorcery or superstition. The following verse confirms this idea:

> Say [O Muḥammad]: 'This is surely my path. I call to God's way—by wholesome discernment [this call is done by] me and by those whosoever follow me. Glory be to God, and I have never been one of the polytheists.'
>
> *The Qurʾān* 12:108

The call to Islam must always be based on logic and reason, to allow man to differentiate between right and wrong. The Islamic Holy Constitution addresses those who have been given reason in this world and who will show remorse in the hereafter when they realize their behaviour was wrong regarding the Islamic call. Consequently, they will be cast into hell.

> Thereupon they said: 'If we had only heard or even rationalized, we would not belong in Hell.'
>
> *The Qur'ān* 67:10

The damned will see that they had not properly used their reason to understand and search for the fact introduced to them. Furthermore, the Islamic Holy Constitution asserts that each individual is fully responsible for his own decision concerning his belief and faith on Resurrection Day, when he will be guided by the way in which he had chosen beforehand.

> Say: 'O Mankind, fact has been revealed to you from God [in accordance with your reason]; whosoever receives guidance does so only for his own benefit, and whosoever goes astray does only for his own benefit too. And I [Muḥammad] am not a guardian over you'.
>
> *The Qur'ān* 10:108

From the above verse, freedom of faith can be derived, but it also assures for each individual a rational responsibility for the conduct concerning his own belief in the light of fact based on pure reason.

The relationship, though, between reason and Divine Law can be summed up by the following questions. Does empirical research in the text of the Islamic Holy Constitution prove or lead to any discrepancy between reason and empirical perception? Is human law covered by the Islamic Holy Constitution as comprehensively as Divine Law? The Islamic Holy Constitution is based not merely on sound reson, but on the sequences of human psychological experience as well.

Many examples reveal that laws outside customary behaviour are difficult to enforce. A classic example is the prohibition of the sale of alcoholic beverages in the United States and the prompt and unanticipated public reaction to the law, which was then invalidated.

The problem of alcoholic consumption encountered at the time of the revelation of the Islamic Holy Constitution occurred because most believers were accustomed to drinking. The problem was rationally and psychologically resolved in stages. During the first phase the Islamic Holy Constitution did not prohibit the use of alcoholic beverages, but indicated that the damage done by and the sins resulting from the drinking of alcohol outweigh its benefits (*The Holy Qur'ān* 2:219). Some believers abstained immediately. The second phase of the issue arose when a drunk believer misread a verse of the Islamic Holy Constitution in his prayer. It was immediately ruled that drinking must be prohibited while prayers are performed (*The Holy Qur'ān* 4:43). As a result of this second provision, more believers ceased using alcohol, while others still found time between prayers to continue to drink. Finally, a complete prohibition was proposed. It was reported the streets of Medina were flooded with wine as every Muslim household was made rid of that beverage; there was no need for inspectors to search (*The Holy Qur'ān* 5:90–1; al-Ṭabarī, 1968, Vol. 7, pp. 31–5).

The Islamic Holy Constitution has pointed out precisely those areas where human reason should be utilized. It proclaims:

> ... Nothing is equivalent to Him [God]. He is the One, the Hearer, the Seer.
>
> *The Qur'ān* 42:11

This verse implicitly enjoins human beings not to employ their reason to analyse that which they cannot see but can only perceive by the evidence of reality. We cannot see God, as we cannot see everything. We know about such reality, but we also believe in many things which cannot be seen but which can be perceived from circumstantial evidence. For instance, we believe that rational people have reason, while at the same time we cannot see or perceive that thing in their body which is called 'reason'. Yet we usually assume from observing the conduct of a person that he or she possesses reason. In this respect, the Islamic Holy Constitution calls for human reason not to be utilized in defining God Himself but in contemplating and exploring the universe's delicate system or the conduct of God in furnishing this same system as a tangible reality through which man can refer to Him. Twentieth-century knowledge reveals that nothing in this universe has been created haphazardly; every single item or function is based on a certain refined system which man is still discovering and pondering over each day.

As a result of this orientation of human reason, nothing prevents any researcher from performing a rational inquiry into the Islamic Holy Constitution. But such a researcher can never do so without giving up all preconceived notions. The goal of the researcher should be to come to know the absolute facts about Islam as a system of living; he should seek these facts in the same manner that scientists perform experiments. The Islamic Holy Constitution both urges and appreciates all sorts of research, analysis and scrutiny which holds as its primary goal the discovery of facts and truth for the welfare of mankind.

We have seen in the preceding verses how the Islamic Holy Constitution encourages human beings to search and to increase their knowledge of all aspects of their condition, through reading, observing, and contemplation. The following verse is a challenge to human reason, in that without knowledge man cannot escape his environmental limits:

> O Community of Jinn and of Men, if you can penetrate the diameters of the heavens and the earth, do then so penetrate. You cannot so penetrate without a positive pretext of knowledge.
>
> *The Qur'ān* 55:33

This verse asserts that the human rational faculty is unlimited, assuming that man can know, see and otherwise perceive knowledge of any scientific subject. It is not the intention of man's faculty of reason to assert or to reject any scientific theory still under rational investigation as fact or fiction. However, looking for absolute fact in any field of knowledge requires a mind free from preconceptions or from a sovereign's direction other than 'to know'. The verse following the one quoted above indicates that man's penetration of the earth's and the heaven's diameters is limited at a point where probing into forbidden knowledge is restricted: any attempt to enter into that area will be met with instant destruction (*The Qur'ān* 55:35).

Before concluding this section, we should question philosophers' thoughts about reason and their theories of knowledge or what has been known as 'epistemology'. Since the first generation of Greek philosophers, attempts have been made to develop a theory of knowledge to account for the source, basis and certainty of man's knowledge. The first theoreticians, the rationalists, tried to find a complete and certain foundation of knowledge in terms of the procedures of human reason. They sought knowledge in the a priori sense—that is, in the sense that no knowledge under any circumstances could be false. Usually the rationalists found that such knowledge could not be discovered through sensory experience, but that it resided in some mental realm. One of the relatively modern advocates of this thought, Rene Descartes, believed that knowledge from the senses was deceitful. The only information he found to be true was the simple statement, 'I exist'. His contention was that he, by inspecting the one truth, 'I think, therefore I exist', had discovered a rule or criterion about all truths. Accordingly, Descartes judged that 'whatever is clearly and distinctly conceived is true' (Popkin and Stroll, 1956, pp. 180–90).

It is not the intention of this book to address the 'rationalist' issue in any great depth, but to analyse briefly Descartes's thought and his famous phrase. A critical examination of both parts of the Descartes statement indicates that each part seems, if not actually equivalent to the other, certainly not to be preceded by the other—simply because thinking derives its activity from the existence which precedes it and not vice-versa. Consequently, it is also true to say, 'I exist; therefore, I think'. On the other hand Descartes, regardless of his elaborate explanation of man's thinking process, did not explicitly point out the physical instruments man uses in the process of thought. Nor, finally, must these instruments be seen in order for man to believe that there is something called 'reason'. No positive knowledge exists to indicate that thinking is performed by the brain alone. One can definitely observe that during the thinking process all of man's natural instincts have to cease temporarily. In addition, the nervous and all other systems of the human body are affected by the thinking process. Surely, then, it cannot be the brain alone which performs the functions of thought. Generally, rationalists assert that by employing certain procedures based on reason alone man can discover valid knowledge—knowledge that can under no circumstances prove false (Popkin and Stroll, 1956, p. 189).

As a result of the 'machine age', other philosophers challenged the rationalists. John Locke, David Hume and Immanuel Kant relied on experience as the source of knowledge, and almost abolished the notion of mind altogether. Kant, in the *Critique of Pure Reason*, tried to reconcile idealistic rationalism and empirical sensualism. He based such a reconciliation on the notion of sense experience as conditioned by the constitution of the human mind, which he assumed contained certain forms of cognition or understanding by which the fleeting impressions of the senses are absorbed, co-ordinated and integrated (Kant, 1900, especially the Preface and 'Transcendental Doctrine of Method', pp. 397–467; *see also* Wilkerson, 1976).

In its Holy Constitution, Islam, some fourteen centuries ago, called for the employment of both ways for understanding the variety of knowledge that man has developed, urging man to utilize both idealistic rationalism and empirical sensualism in accordance with the requirements of each specific field of knowledge.

The Islamic Holy Constitution and Ethics

Ethics is the study of human conduct, not by itself but as it relates to certain basic ideals and norms. Moral philosophers consider these ideals and norms to be the expression of certain fundamental presuppositions that every individual accepts as valid. For this particular reason ethics is usually called a 'normative' science, as distinct from such 'positive' sciences as psychology or sociology. Although the latter concern themselves with human behaviour, psychology focuses on an individual's mental processes while sociology addresses ethics in relation to the physical and social environments in which an individual is placed. For psychology, all the studies of behaviour are the same, whether the subject of research is a criminal or a saint. In ethics, however, the cases of study are each completely different. The saint, for example, illustrates the ideal pattern of conduct while the criminal is expected to correct his behaviour to that of the ideal pattern.

Most moral philosophers assume that ethics specifies current moral conceptions to unfold their ultimate presuppositions. However, the still unsettled controversies among moral philosophers started with differences in their conception of *summum bonum* (the greatest good) and the ideal of happiness. Those who advocate the greatest good for happiness reject the notion of basic presuppositions and try to confine the study of ethics to the following four basic questions:

1. What is the greatest good in human conduct?
2. What are the sources of man's knowledge of right and wrong?
3. What are the sanctions of moral conduct?
4. What are the motives which encourage an individual to perform moral acts?

The question that arose initially was if ethics philosophers accept human happiness as their ultimate goal, then what varieties of happiness should be pursued—egoism or altruism; hedonism or utilitarianism? No clearcut choice exists. Advocates of each of these 'isms' have strongly supported their own doctrines and not that of the others (Dar, 1969, pp. 1–6).

Islam considers ethics and moral conduct as important aspects, as part of a necessary and basic condition in accepting, both individually and collectively, the practice of Islam. Since ethics and moral conduct are broad topics that can take volumes of discussion, this book only outlines the basic concepts of this phenomenon.

Ethics and moral conduct in Islam have been situated midway between the two extremes of the presupposition and the greatest good regarding what constitutes happiness. The Islamic Holy Constitution proclaims, as the Prophet says:

> He will never be a believer who does not love for his brother what he loves for himself.
>
> Al-Bukhārī, *Īmān* 7, 71, 72

This verse from the Sunnah indicates that initially human conduct is either right or wrong. The verse also implies a frank answer to the four questions listed above. It defines the greatest good, the source of man's knowledge of right and wrong, the sanctions of moral conduct and, finally, the motivation behind human performance of that conduct. To explain these phenomena, the verse recognizes that reason must be the only source for determining the greatest good. What is 'right' for someone must likewise be 'right' for another and vice-versa. At this point, the verse does not define any right or wrong itself because of the implicit assumption of universal standards. These common rights and wrongs serve as antidotes for mankind in various circumstances. Moreover, every society within the Islamic Nation would maintain certain of its own norms and traditions which do not contradict the framework of the Islamic Holy Constitution and which would have to be accepted as ethical norms peculiar to each specific society. So, the behaviour, which seems right for someone and which may seem wrong or at least uncomfortable for another, must be measured by such universal standards of wrong and right. The ultimate sanction of moral conduct lies within the individual; thus, any human who does not wish to be harmed must not think of harming others. Such a standard should also provide the personal motivation for human moral conduct. However other patterns can be extracted from the above verse, which also indicates that no end ever justifies any means and suggests that behaviour toward others must reflect the very basis of the human relationship with God. Human moral conduct must, therefore, be a criterion of belief and reflect a confidential relationship with God Who otherwise will not accept any religious practice based on immoral behaviour toward His honoured children.

Although the Islamic Holy Constitution recognizes reason as the principle tool for determining the greatest good, it provides Muslims with examples to follow and to use as models for resolving misunderstandings or disputes. The Prophet of Islam has been introduced in the Islamic Holy Constitution as an example of perfect human moral conduct and behaviour.

> Surely, you are on the mighty, firm ground of developed ethics.
>
> *The Qurʾān* 68:4

Taking this clue as unequivocal reason, Muslims concluded that the Prophet's moral conduct is an integral part of the Islamic Holy Constitution, with the exception of what has been explicitly prescribed for him as special conduct for his prophecy. Consequently, since the first generation of Islam, Muslims have emulated the Prophet's behaviour as an example of human perfection. Yet no Muslim has ever claimed that he could follow precisely that highly developed moral conduct, simply because it is extremely difficult for ordinary people to live in accordance with the Prophet's behaviour. For instance, in his period of prophecy, the Prophet never used the word 'no' to reject someone, or to refuse any request (Muslim, *Faḍāʾil*, 56). The Islamic Holy Constitution considers human happiness to be a combination of moral or ethical conduct in this life with a reward in the next. More significantly, the Islamic Holy Constitution equates personal conduct with one's personal relationship with God. Any practice of the Islamic religion deriving from immoral behaviour will not be accepted.

Sovereignty in Islam

The concepts of both 'state' and 'sovereignty' have retained their secular connotations to replace the basis of tyranny practised by the priestly class in the name of religion and by the Divine Right of kings in mediaeval Europe. Both concepts came into use at about the same time. In Europe, the concept of sovereignty originally derived from the dispute between popes and emperors. The papal/imperial controversies were not, in fact, about sovereignty but, in most cases, about political predominance. Mediaeval political thought was inherently both constitutional and hierarchical. The rights and duties of kings were all proper matters for dispute but almost all disputants agreed that such features were bound by eternal, divine, natural and positive law. However, the concept of sovereignty denotes a theory of politics, maintaining that every system of government must grant either an individual or a body of people the absolute power to exercise the final judgement or decision. Such a person or body must be recognized both as competent to decide and able to enforce decisions. Although it is clear that the debate about sovereignty has been historically exhausted, the theory did fulfill a particular need in Europe in the sixteenth and seventeenth centuries. Thus, the phenomenon and concept of sovereignty are best understood historically. They originated as an expression of the need to find a purely secular basis for authority amid the emerging European states' organizations of that time.

According to Sir William Blackstone, every state must possess a supreme, irresistible, absolute and uncontrolled authority in which the *jura summa imperii*, or the right of sovereignty, resides. This supreme authority is usually differently vested from one state to another and could be shared by more than one person or body of governmental orders. For instance, the constitution of Great Britain indicates that the supreme authority is vested in the King, Lords and Commons (Blackstone, 1783, Vol. 1, Chapters 1–2; Vol. 2, Chapter 1). However, Blackstone's assertion was rejected by Jeremy Bentham, who exposed and ridiculed its fallacy. Bentham explained that the theory of sovereignty is much more plausible as a prescriptive rather than as a descriptive proposition, that states lacking sovereignty commonly find themselves in difficulties, both in matters of defense and in the resolution of their conflicts (Parekh, 1973, pp. 175–94, 257–90).

Jean Bodin and Thomas Hobbes, both considered prime exponents of sovereignty, have similar, if not the same thoughts as those that have been spelled out by the famous Islamic theologians—the Muʿtazilites and the ʾAshʿarites, especially regarding the basis of right and wrong. Hobbes asserted that there is no right and wrong until the sovereign makes a law creating such a distinction (Hobbes, 1965, Chapters 14, 17, 18). Centuries before Hobbes the ʾAshʿarites had already explained this theme and added that the sovereign must be God alone (Al-Ashʿarī, 1969, Vol. 1, 345–52). Bodin, however, tried to bind his sovereign by natural law and by laws declared by God (Bodin, 1967, Book 1, Chapters 8–10). The Muʿtazilite adhered to this doctrine, but added that both natural law and the law of God must be tempered by human reason (Al-Ashʿarī, 1969, Vol. 1, pp. 235–80). According to Bernard Crick, both Bodin and Hobbes, in attempting to formulate their theories about sovereignty, 'were preoccupied with the problem of civil war'. Hence, their notions 'are appropriate to the state of emergency' (Crick, 1968, p. 79). The essence of sovereignty is the power of command and such a command must issue from a single will.

In general, the modern thinking concerning the concept of sovereignty may not essentially differ from that of Islamic political theorists. The Islamic Holy Constitution declared the essence of sovereignty to be the power to command and this supreme power always to belong to God Himself and to His revealed messages.

> Verily, the only sovereign is God. He declares the law and He is the best judge.
>
> *The Qur'ān* 6:57

> For He only is the sovereign, and He is the Swiftest of Reckoners.
>
> *The Qur'ān* 6:62

> Surely, the only sovereign is God, He has commanded that you worship no one but Him.
>
> *The Qur'ān* 12:40

> Everything [that exists] will perish except His countenance. To Him belongs sovereignty and to Him you will be returned.
>
> *The Qur'ān* 28:88

These verses confirm that in the Islamic system the absolute sovereign is God alone and by extension sovereignty belongs to His final revealed message of Islam as Muslims believe. However, the Islamic Holy Constitution has bestowed upon the Islamic Nation and upon its leadership a special sovereign power to be exercised when necessary.

Clearly, the Islamic Nation has been given the right to select or 'the power to choose' its own leadership from among its members:

> ... their ruling system is based on the right of *shūrā* amongst them [that is, either by consensus or election], and from what We have provided them they outlay [to the poor].
>
> *The Qur'ān* 42:38

The power to choose its leadership is one characteristic that distinguishes the Islamic Nation.

The Islamic Holy Constitution does not provide specific details about suffrage or procedures for the election of leaders. The features of the election are ignored deliberately, thus providing an opportunity to develop the procedures or laws to regulate the sovereign power bestowed upon the Islamic Nation in accordance with its circumstances and exigencies. The election process is always supposed to reflect equality and justice. However, the election regulations must never be considered a part of the Islamic Holy Constitution, because they are always susceptible to change according to the prevailing situation. The procedures used to elect the first four Right-guided Caliphs during the early decades of the first Islamic century are not by any means acceptable in the modern fifteenth century of the Islamic era. If the situation were stable and predictable and the election procedures not liable to develop or change, the Islamic Holy Constitution would not have hesitated to prescribe full details to regulate an election.

The other sovereign power that has been vested in the leaders of the Islamic Nation by the Islamic Holy Constitution is of two sorts. The first is that the final, irresistible and absolute authority should be vested in the head of the Islamic Nation by the Islamic Holy Constitution:

> . . . and discuss in deliberation with them [the professional Muslims] the governmental affairs thereupon, whenever you [single pronoun] decide then [carry out your decision and] place your confidence and trust in God, verily God loves those who are trusting Him.
>
> *The Qur'ān* 3:159

According to this verse, the head of the Islamic state is the final authority in the Islamic Nation. The only control over him is the Islamic Congress. He is ordered by the Islamic Holy Constitution to review with the Islamic Congress all aspects of each situation before making his final decision. However, once he decides, his decision must be final and absolute and must be carried out by the whole nation unless it is contrary to a clear version of the Islamic Holy Constitution in the normal circumstances.

Secondly, the leaders of the Islamic State have been given the ultimate authority by the Islamic Holy Constitution to exercise and execute the Islamic Holy Constitution, the Constitutional Law and the state laws that are not explicitly outlined. The Islamic Holy Constitution has declared another order for the Islamic Nation:

> O, you who believe, obey God, and obey the Prophet and those

> who are in power amongst you. Thereupon, if you have any matter of dispute refer it to the God and to the Prophet (that is, the Islamic Holy Constitution) if you certainly believe in God and the Last Day, that is the best deed and it is better to interpret
>
> *The Qur'ān* 4:59

The Islamic Nation, collectively and individually, has to obey fully the Islamic Holy Constitution, and in the same degree the state enacts laws that are recognized in the cited verse ('and those who are in power amongst you'). Meanwhile, no belligerent act is permitted against the elected authority as long as it does not deviate from the basic instructions of the Islamic Holy Constitution. The verse above emphasizes the obedience and compliance of the believers toward their leaders. Whenever a dispute arises, the Islamic Holy Constitution must be the first and last source to which they turn for judgement.

In summary, fourteen centuries ago, the Islamic Holy Constitution proclaimed that 'only the laws are sovereign'. This proclamation is designed to be the first step toward a democratic and liberal society. Islam delineates the basic elements for a democratic government that is to be elected by the Islamic Nation. The Islamic Holy Constitution recognizes the need for state law to cover those areas that may not otherwise have been covered. Certain sovereign power and authority is given to both the Islamic Nation and its leaders to exercise and execute the Islamic Holy Constitution. The Islamic Nation has been instructed to obey fully the state-enacted laws unless they deviate from the Islamic Holy Constitution's guidance.

2

The Basic Foundations of the Islamic Political System

The most striking phenomenon of human existence is development and change, through which man has been able to build his civilization in ordered stages. Of the crucial factors in development trends, perhaps the key role is played by the dynamic interaction between the infrastructure and the superstructure of laws. The maintaining of the *status quo* in the superstructure of law has normally led nations to stasis and stagnation, but dynamic evolution in nations' lives requires constant modification to promote and introduce a new national spirit and, in turn, to preserve and guard the dynamism toward more advanced stages of civilization.

Although it is generally accepted that Islam has precisely regulated all aspects of its followers' lives—religious, social, political—without exception, the Islamic Holy Constitution takes account of the necessity for change and development and, in consequence, never gives precise instruction in the areas of law that are subject to alteration in accordance with changing circumstances. The infrastructure laws, such as the Divine Services and personal statutes, are comprehensively decided and regulated, but the Islamic Holy Constitution has merely drawn basic outlines or given clues for the superstructure laws that are always subject to change according to prevailing circumstances. Even with the latter, however, there may be found precise details about minute points that are constant and not subject to development.

The reason for this division in instructing Muslims is to ensure the continuity of the Islamic system. If the Islamic Holy Constitution had given precise instructions in all areas, Islam would have survived only in certain times and places, whereas the continuity of a system is governed mostly by its ability to change continuously and by its responsiveness to varying conditions.

The Islamic political system is one in which most regulations are liable to change; however, within it there are particular points that are precisely regulated because of their permanent universality. Thus, suitable instruction for every aspect of Muslims' lives can be found in the Islamic Holy Constitution. Detailed instructions are provided in cases where the situation is universally applicable, while brief outlines are given in situations that are subject to change. Such consideration for the circumstances and instruction in the Islamic system means that the Islamic Holy Constitution is promulgated by God, the One Whose knowledge is not restricted to time or place and that the system is permanent and universal.

The Islamic Holy Constitution has prescribed basic guidelines to enhance Muslims' freedom to enact laws to suit their special conditions throughout future times. The basic features of the Islamic political system are equality, justice, freedom, Muslim nationality, and the status of non-Muslims under the Islamic system.

Equality in Islam

The term 'equality' has been much overused and exploited in the history of ideas and governing institutions. Both philosophers and statesmen have employed it in accordance with their own ideals or to justify their action as rulers.

Three famous equivoques have been invented to assert the absolute equality of mankind: men are equal, men have the right to be treated equally, and men are created equal. The difficulty, however, is to define the important characteristics that all men possess in precisely the same degree so that, whatever their other differences, their equality might be justified. This fundamental equality, then, would make men equal. According to Arnold Brecht, philosophers have scientifically 'failed to offer a yardstick by which the relative weight [of human equality] could be measured' (Brecht, 1959, p. 306). Brecht scientifically examines all characteristics introduced by philosophers and thinkers to support their notion of equality, but the results revealed that all these traits are invalid. He also asserts that 'equality entered the picture [of political and economic thought] only as a late comer in the French Revolution; it met with a great deal of suspicion and resistance not merely in practice but also in philosophy' (Brecht, 1959, p. 313). At any rate, the controversy over equality arose, not for the sake of mankind, but to support certain idealistic or political goals.

The ideas of equality and inequality have been carefully addressed by the Islamic Holy Constitution:

> O, mankind, verily We created you from a single male and female, and rendered you nations and tribes for knowing. Surely the noblest of you in the sight of God is the most pious one. Thereupon God is Omniscient and Expert
>
> *The Qur'ān* 49:13

Usually the Islamic Holy Constitution addresses 'mankind', rather than Muslims alone, when it wants to focus attention on general facts or natural laws, as in the verse above. It reflects one of the most striking characteristics concerning human equality, a characteristic that may not be referred to by any other work, and denotes a phenomenon that all human beings shared equally. This distinctive characteristic is the ability of mankind to communicate with each other—'to speak', 'to write' and 'to read'—one o the most significant features of human beings. Undoubtedly, without communication or the movement of knowledge, no civilization could ever exist.

The Islamic Holy Constitution has precisely professed man's measured equality, his ability to know and to transmit his knowledge to others. This characteristic of 'knowing' comprises the basic feature of human equality regardless of his other differences or handicaps. For example, even though humans speak different languages, every individual is able to master one or more languages other than his own. Consequently, regardless of any natural differences (sex, colour, character, human traits, natural endowments) and institutional variations (citizenship, religion, social rank), man is equal in his ability to know and to communicate his knowledge.

However, the Islamic Holy Constitution does not consider this type of equality to entitle man to be absolutely equal. As mankind will never be entirely and unrestrictedly equal, the Islamic Holy Constitution declares that natural human inequalities must be recognized:

> Say: Are they equal—those who know and those who do not know? Only those who are highly rational recognize [this fact].
>
> *The Qur'ān* 39:9

The verse emphasizes the inequality between men in regard to natural endowments, the differences among human beings readily apparent to all. Without specifying what type of knowledge, the verse simply refers to the inequality between those who know and those who do not. It may be concluded that every human being has certain abilities and interests dictated by his own nature. No equality should be claimed between specialists in one field of knowledge, let alone in different ones. The generally accepted belief, that every individual or group sharing a similar variety of knowledge should enjoy a certain status in society with regard to class, income and performance, is probably not the standard that must be recognized by the Islamic Holy Constitution because of the inequality in their ability and performance.

The Islamic Holy Constitution has recognized and taken special notice of the equality of mankind in general. Some examples explain the view of the Islamic Holy Constitution.

The first example is equality regarding the right of all men to be protected and to live securely with their property. No one should pose a threat to any individual without the due process of law:

> Do not kill a man whose soul [nafs] has been made sacred, except through the due process of law.
>
> *The Qurʾān* 6:151

> Therefore, We [God] have foreordained to the sons of Israel that whosoever kills a human being [soul] without [any lawful reason such as due to] the man's slaughtering or corruption in the earth, it is as though he has killed all mankind. And, whosoever saves a life, it is as though he has saved the lives of all mankind. Our prophets have already come to them with clear verses and signs, but many of them have afterward become excessively corrupt on the earth.
>
> The only recompense of those who declare war against God and His Prophet [referring to those who kill and grow corrupt on the earth] is this: They are to be killed or crucified, or their hand and feet alternately mutilated, or they are to be expatriated from the land. That is the degradation for them in this world, and they will have a mighty chastisement in the hereafter.
>
> But those who repent before you are able to introduce them to the process of law, thereupon you should know that God is All-Forgiving, All-Compassionate.
>
> *The Qurʾān* 5:32–34

The Prophet has also spoken on this point:

> The greatest sins, which will not be tolerated or forgiven on the Resurrection Day, are those of associating a god with God and those of killing a human being (nafs) without due process of law.
>
> Al-Bukhārī, *Hudūd*, 44; Muslim, *Īmān* 144–5

As a special caution to Muslims who might think that killing non Muslims is allowable, the Islamic Holy Constitution has declared in the verse of Sunnah:

> The believer still has an opportunity in his religion [that God may forgive his sins] unless he kills without lawful reason.
>
> *Al-Bukhārī, Diyyāt* 1

Before explaining these verses, it should be noted that the Islamic Holy Constitution, in relation to this context, almost always uses the word 'nafs' (soul) for a human being without any distinction as to religion, colour, race or sex. The equality and sacredness of the human soul is recognized and mandated by the Islamic Holy Constitution. Moreover, unlawful killing is considered an act of war against God Himself and His Prophets. Therefore, the Islamic Holy Constitution emphasizes the equality of all human beings in respect to the sacredness of their lives and states that they deserve equality of protection. Protection of life and property is so important that any threat to such security requires severe punishment in God's name. Thus no one, whatever his status, power or wealth, should ever think of committing any crime that would menace, threaten, or blackmail a human being or his property. However, the unequivocal humanitarian aspect of the Islamic Holy Constitution includes an appeal to pardon those who may repent before the existing authority is able to prosecute them; both authority and society have to allow repenters another chance to become contributing members of society without considering their dark past.

The second example concerns the equality of all men before the law. Many verses of the Islamic Holy Constitution and examples of the early practice of the Companions of the Prophet can be applied here. In one famous episode of the Sunnah, one of the most relevant verses, it was related that:

> The nobles of Quraysh once feared that legal punishment would be

> inflicted on a lady of Banī Makhzūm, who committed theft. They discussed the matter amongst themselves because she belonged to a high ranking branch of the Qurayshite tribe. Their fallacious hope was to save her from legal penalty. But, who dared to talk to the Prophet in her case? One of them suggested 'Usāmah, the favorite of the Prophet. 'Usāmah accepted the mission, but when the Prophet heard him, he exasperatedly said. 'Do you intercede [with me] to violate one of the legal punishments of God?'—Then the Prophet stood up and addressed the people, saying: 'O people, nations before you were destroyed and went astray because when a noble person committed a crime they did not apply the law to him but when an ordinary man committed the same crime they inflicted the legal penalty on him. I swear by God if Fāṭimah the daughter of Muḥammad [referring to his own daughter] commits theft, Muḥammad will cut off her hand.'
>
> Al-Bukhārī, *Hudūd*, 13

This verse is so clear that it needs no explanation. It decrees that all human beings are equal or must be treated equally before the law and no one, no matter of what social or political status, is immune from legal punishment.

In summary, these two examples represent the most significant aspects of the equality of men. Of course, social services such as education, health services and equality of opportunity to earn social rank, must be recognized by the authority of the Islamic State along with the acknowledgement of the inequality of men as a result of natural endowments. The Islamic Holy Constitution is moderate in this respect and addresses, in a rational fashion, the issues of human equality and inequality, not accepting either radical extreme.

Justice in Islam

What is just? What is unjust? These questions are the basis for political and judicial thought. The laws laid down by governments ought to be just, and they ought to be administered fairly. Lawyers' minds have generally been fixed on the second question; political scientists, on the first. However, the basic questions are the same: what is just? and what is unjust?

These questions presuppose conflicts of interest. Justice presupposes people pressing claims and justifying them by rules or standards (Brecht, 1959, pp. 136–7), distinguishing justice from charity, benevolence or generosity. This approach is reason to question distributive justice, the ensuing problem of allocation of rights and benefits. Nevertheless, giving judgement in favour of one party has this in common with distribution—they all may involve overriding a claim and treating one party more or less harshly than another. Philosophers recognize three sources that may determine the just and unjust: God, nature and reason. However, there is as yet no agreement as to which may give a precise answer.

The principles of justice, such as impartiality of the judge and/or the equality or inequality of participants or cases, are not limited to the law. Justice, in fact, should be regarded, as the philosophers indicate, as a characteristic of all moral judgement; the agent must place his own interest on the same level as the interest of others affected by the judge's decision (Brecht, 1959, pp. 138–62). In common usage, justice still retains significant traces of its original comprehensiveness. For this reason, the very broad concept of justice presented in God's messages and in philosophers' works continues to be important.

The Islamic Holy Constitution has placed significant emphasis on justice as one of the most important aspects of personal faith, because of its deep involvement with the moral values of ideological belief. The broad concept of justice presented and dealt with in the Islamic Holy Constitution is an extensive topic and, because of this, only an outline will be presented in this book to show how justice is relevantly connected to personal faith in God. Even though the Islamic Holy Constitution has spelled out many examples of justice and injustice in different events or stories and it contains strict regulations concerning certain capital crimes, there has not been a clear definition of what is just and what is unjust. Because the aspect of justice cannot be precisely and materially defined, it has been emphatically connected with individual faith and moral conduct. Thus, the Islamic Holy Constitution has declared in the Prophetic Sunnah that:

> He will never be a believer, who does not love for his brother whatsoever he loves for himself.
>
> Al-Bukhārī, *Īmān*, 7

This general measurement of personal faith indicates that justice can not be conceptualized materially by a precise definition. Moreover, each aspect of justice has so many different phases that can be determined only by circumstantial evidence and not by plain definition.

Regardless of this ambiguity concerning justice, the command for justice has to come directly from God Himself, instructing mankind to act justly towards each individual as a person engaged with others in joint practices designed to promote common or complementary interests. The following verses delineate this basic element of justice:

> Verily, God has commanded justice, performance of good deeds, and giving to kinsmen. And He has proscribed abomination, reprehensible action, and whoredom. He is admonishing you so that you may haply remember.
>
> *The Qur'ān* 16:90

> O, you who believe, be upright and steadfast in justice, witnessing for God, even though it be against yourselves, parents and kinsmen. God is more entitled to them whether each of them is rich or poor. Therefore, do not follow caprice lest it cause you to lapse from justice. But if you lapse or fall away [from being just], God is Expert of what you are doing.
>
> *The Qur'ān* 4:135

> O, you who believe, be steadfast witnesses of God in justice, and let not the hatefulness of people [results of their bad deeds and behaviors] seduce you to deal with them unjustly. Be just [in all circumstances] that is the nearest to piousness, have fear of God. Surely, God is expert of what you are doing.
>
> *The Qur'ān* 5:8

These Qur'ānic verses of the Islamic Holy Constitution define the concept of justice in Islam as an integrated phase of faith. Although the first verse differentiates between charity and justice, it indicates one of the general and direct orders of God Himself, i.e. the quality of justice demonstrates an individual's faith in God's message—Islam.

In the second verse the concept of justice is regarded as the deposition of God Himself. For this type of testimonial to the Diety, one has to be just even against oneself, parents and kinsmen, whatever the situation of power or wealth. A Muslim must fulfil the ideal of justice without considering any relationship or social rank; by doing so he accepts the heavy mission to be a witness of God. This duty is more than an honorable task designed for the Muslim; it is an obligatory order for which the believer will be accountable in the hereafter.

The third verse repeatedly emphasizes that the Muslim must always witness for God in justice, for to spread justice in the world is one of the most significant missions of Muslims on earth. The idea of justice as a reciprocal requirement—returning evil for evil as much as good for good—must be emphatically banished from Muslims' minds. The hatred of people who practice evil must not stimulate Muslims to exploit the opportunity by acting unjustly. Justice has to appear as a sign of Islam in Muslims' behaviour to distinguish them from other people; this sign is a great step in the stages of faith that will steer Muslims towards human perfection.

The Islamic Holy Constitution directs Muslim attention towards another aspect of justice: the role of judgeship. It orders those who are involved in making judgements between people to judge justly:

> God commands you to deliver the trusts back to their owners alone, and when you judge between mankind that you must judge justly. God reminds you with good admonitions, God is ever Hearer, Seer.
>
> *The Qur'ān* 4.58

In this respect, the Islamic Holy Constitution also relates that an eloquent plaintiff may delude the judge by presenting his side logically. The story of Prophet Dāwūd (David) directs Muslims' attention to this kind of delusion. The story says that while the Prophet David was in his prayer niche, two men jumped down to him, stating they were plaintiffs and one of them was outraged by the other. They requested Prophet David to judge their case justly. One of them eloquently and logically presented his side, saying that his brother owned ninety-nine ewes and he owned only one: but his brother was tenaciously begging him to join this ewe with the others. Since the case was so logically developed by one side, Prophet David immediately and unexpectedly issued his judgement stating, 'Your brother has ill-treated you by asking your partnership'. Prophet David then explained the disadvantage of this type of partnership. Thereupon came a direct revelation to Prophet David indicating that he was chosen to be a Caliph to judge between people justly. But following the above pattern in any judgement leads certainly to caprice; Prophet David heard only from one party and issued his decision, whereas justice requires that he should have heard from the other parties involved before making a decision (*The Qur'ān* 38:21–6).

Justice accordingly is an aspect of moral conduct and whatever procedures are developed to rule justly, the judge may wrongly issue his decision while thinking he is right. The Prophet of Islam has emphasized this phase of justice to warn those who are trying to present their case in such a way to confuse the judge.

> Verily, you come to me with your legal cases; and probably some of you present his case more eloquently than the other. For the sake of God I am but a human being, I will judge according to what I hear. Therefore, any one I accordingly give him the legal right of the other; I am giving him an appropriate place in Hell, if he want to take it or leave it.
>
> Al-Bukhārī, *Aḥkām*, 20

Finally, the answers to the question of just and unjust are morally conceptualized because justice is basically derived from a factor of consciousness, which is usually exhibited through the emotional and spiritual impetus of the individual's ideological belief. Thus Islam posits the concept of justice as an integral part of personal faith in God's message—Islam.

Freedom in Islam

Historically, philosophers and social thinkers have specifically used the term 'freedom' as a moral and social concept to refer either to circumstances which arise in the relationship between men, or to a specific predicament of social life. Even when so restricted, important differences of usage are possible and most of the political or philosophical argument about the meaning or the nature of freedom is concerned with the legitimacy or appropriateness of a particular application of the term.

The concept of freedom has been central in European individualism and liberalism. According to this tradition, freedom denotes primarily a condition characterized by the absence of coercion or constraint imposed by another person (Oppenheim, 1961, pp. 33–7). An important point appears in Bertrand Russell's often quoted statement, 'Freedom in general, may be defined as the absence of obstacles to the realization of desires' (Russell, 1941, p. 251). This statement hardly goes far enough to indicate unlimited constraint over man's exercise of choice. However, freedom as a state of mind must be distinguished from freedom as a state of affairs.

In Islam, the concept of freedom basically stands for the ultimate responsibility of man. The famous phrase, 'if you are responsible, you are free', significantly corresponds to the Islamic system's appplication of the concept of freedom. From its outset Islam has recognized freedom of belief or thought, which is ideologically the significant foundation of the concept of freedom. An individual without such an ideological belief is still in the chaotic stage, but when he holds or professes any sort of ideology it seems that his concept of freedom is determined and influenced by such ideology. With this realization Islam, as a systematic theology, has considered itself a memento, for those who have the will to contemplate its teaching rationally. Islam is not, by any means, an enforceable dogmatic ideology to be followed blindly or even supported by polemical logic.

The Islamic Holy Constitution has emphatically declared on many occasions that each individual is fully and discernibly responsible for deciding his own destiny. He has to choose freely the path to follow. Such a choice or decision is the most significant aspect of freedom in an individual life, influencing and directing the individual throughout the whole life. Meanwhile, the individual will be completely responsible for his acts and behaviour which will be regulated by what he has chosen, both in this life and in the hereafter. The idea of freedom of thought or belief and individual responsibility is delineated by the Islamic Holy Constitution in many Qur'ānic verses, of which the following are good examples:

> Whatever a person has earned will be credited on his record. And, nobody will be held responsible for another's load; then to your God you will return and He will notify you of that wherein you differed.
>
> *The Qur'ān* 6:164

> He frowned [the Prophet Muḥammad] and turned away, when the blind [man] came to him.
>
> And who informs you that he may purify himself [by accepting Islam?]
>
> Or, yet he may remember; thereupon the remainder would turn to his advantage. But, for the one who dispenses with it [Islam], you are impeding his way.

Yet, it is not your task to have him purify [accept Islam].

But, when the one who moves across to you [seeking your guidance] and has fear of [God], you try to avoid him.

No indeed, this is merely a reminder. So let whosoever wills take heed of such a memento.

The Qur'ān 80:1–12

The first quotation indicates one of the starting points of individual responsibility regarding thoughts, beliefs, deeds and acts as long as an individual has the ability to communicate and judge rationally. Thus, before a person restricts himself to any certain ideology, he has full freedom to decide which path to follow. However, once the decision is made, he must carry out his ideological belief and fulfill all the obligatory tasks. In Islam, such a person is no longer in a chaotic stage. He is, in effect, influenced rationally by the tenet he has chosen. He is no longer acting as an animal, eating, drinking and waiting for his irrevocable fate.

The second group of verses relates one of the famous censure parables revealed in the early prophetical period while the Prophet was trying sincerely and carefully to convince one of the leaders of his own people, a blind man came and interrupted him, seeking an explanation about the new faith. The Prophet, irritated by the blind man, frowned and turned away, trying to continue his conversation with the noble man in the endeavor to persuade him to Islam. These verses reprimand and warn the Prophet and, of course, the Muslims that their task is restricted to providing correct information about Islam, not to persuading or forcing people to profess the faith. Islam is a memento to the people who realize the need for it and have the will to look for both spiritual and material guidance based on rational inquiry.

This freedom of choice which is emphasized in many verses of the Islamic Holy Constitution, is one of the most significant factors for the law of apostasy in Islam. Choice of belief or thought is not a game. There must be complete rational and psychological satisfaction with what has been chosen. An individual must realize when professing Islam that he is introducing himself to a complete material and spiritual change in a brand-new milieu of blood kinship, that he agrees to be one with the Muslims more closely than with his own kinsman.

Thus, the law of apostasy is equal to the man-made law of treason, with one important distinction; it is not tantamount to denouncing or breaking with one's country. Renouncing Islam is regarded as a betrayal of faith in God Himself and a denunciation of kinship. Capital punishment is the penalty in man-made law for treasonable action and has become recognized internationally as the norm or standard law for such a crime. However, in Islam man has been treated more humanely and considerable attention is paid to his dignity, which is not regarded in any man-made law. Repentance is required before executing the penalty. Sentence must be delayed for at least three days if there is hope of repentence, even though the penitent is not sincere. Will any sort of man-made law accept such repentence in a case of treason? No such understanding of human weakness has been exhibited among the comunity of nations yet.

Finally, the concept of freedom in Islam is to be considered as the first stage of action towards rationally regulated behaviour and conduct, based on the real need of mankind materially and spiritually. The Islamic Holy Constitution regards the concept of responsibilty and commitment in an individual's life as the keystone in determining the concept of freedom. This responsibility guides an individual away from the chaotic stage and towards a rational stage. However, the concept of freedom is always limited whenever the responsibility is increased and vice versa.

The Nationality of Muslims

The concept of nationalism, with its supported major factors, was initially launched into the world by the Islamic Holy Constitution. When Islam began, almost every existing socity was severely divided into classes, even though the people were descended from the same race. The first and main concept behind the idea of nationalism introduced by Islam was to break up the classes that made some men superior to others by virtue of wealth. To denounce the distinction that existed between the noble or clergy and the layman, Islam has tried to fuse people into one homogeneous nation, adhering to certain socio-political and ideological thought. This is the most important factor in the concept of Islamic nationalism. The other two major factors, language and historical heritage, are carefully designated; the Arabic language was chosen to be the official language of the Islamic Holy Constitution, and the historical events were chosen to represent the history of mankind with, of course, the events associated with the Prophet's lifetime. This socio-political and ideological thought, with one official language and common historical heritage, constitute a certain political unity and entity dubbed the Islamic Nation. The following Sunnah and Qur'ānic verses refer to this distinctive identity.

> This is a Declaration (Kitāb) of Muḥammad the Messenger of God to operate amongst the faithful (mu'minūn) and the submissive to God (Muslimun) from amongst the Quraysh and the people of Yathrib [another name for Medina] and those who may follow and join them [by being Muslims] and take part with them in jihād, verily they constitute 'one nation' distinct from all other people.
>
> *Declaration of Medina*, verse 1

> Verily, this nation of yours constitutes one nation and I am your God, therefore worship Me [alone].
>
> *The Qur'ān* 21:92

> Verily this nation of yours constitutes one nation. and I am your God, be cautious of Me.
>
> *The Qur'ān* 23:52

These three verses assert one absolute fact: the Muslims by the definition of their Constitution are always one nation or one distinguishable political unity. The three major attributes of the idea of nationalism are the system they adhered to, the language of their Islamic Holy Constitution and the historical events related by the Islamic Holy Constitution. In addition, the history of their Prophet and His companions significantly distinguish Muslims from all other nations. So, a Muslim who has accepted Islam as the systemic theology for his life must consider himself accordingly an integrated part of this entity—the Islamic Nation. Even though he may live outside Islamic territorial jurisdiction, he, nevertheless, owes certain duties and obligations towards his Nation as the Nation does to him.

The verses indicate that membership in a society based on shared race, colour, geographical site, language and historical heritage does not constitute as great a bond or produce as homogeneous a society as the attribution to an ideal belief. Material attributions will vanish promptly and be forgotten before any real danger to life or individual interests. This fact has apparently been acknowledged in this modern era where individuals are always guarding their personal interests and completely ignoring their nationality or even their own kin, laying aside their belief.

The above quoted verses call Muslims, who belong and adhere to a certain systematic theology, 'one nation'. The word 'one' has been repeated in the three verses to emphasize the quality of attribution. Therefore the nationality of those who vehemently submit, dedicate and devote their lives to the Islamic system revealed by God to the Prophet Muḥammad, must be Muslim. Their patriotism should be oriented to their system in the first place to fulfill the most important aspect of nationalism, the Brotherhood of Islam. However, genealogical attributions such as tribe, kin or partisanship are acknowledged in the Islamic system to determine the responsibility of wergild in the case of accidental homicide, as the Declaration of Medina indicates.

The slogan of nationalism that arose in Europe in the early seventeenth century, almost caused the destruction of all European communities. However, there would have been a different situation compared to what we see in Europe today if the treaty of 'Westphalia' in 1648 (which confirmed the new principles of 'just equilibrium' among the competing societies of Europe) did not exist. The colonial powers of the early eighteenth century (Britain, France and Germany) realized the great advantage of spreading the concept of nationalism among all ethnic groups in the world, especially within the multiethnic societies of the the Islamic State—Ottoman Empire. Their real goal behind the propagation of such ideas was, and probably still is, to facilitate the continuity of their role in these areas that provide undisputed markets and resources of raw material for their industries. This eminent goal has been enveloped in a splendid covert framework, overtly designed to assist those helpless ethnic groups to have their own state and government influenced by Europe's historical and cultural stereotypes. The implementation of colonial plans was well-prepared: a considerable number of these societies were educated and influenced by the colonialists and subsequently held key positions in their home administrations, working on the behalf of the western countries. In addition, colonial missionaries were sent to these areas and with the full co-operation of the Christians living there and of others who aspired after special privileges participated in the destruction of these poor countries from within. Last but not least, internal factors, such as the decay of the administrations, worked to complete the destruction of the existing Islamic State and prepared the climate for the nationalist revolutions so prevalent in the Ottoman Empire. The most important outcome of these revolutions was their complete loyality to the colonial powers, which was the main reason behind the propagation of the nationalist concept. However the plan to accomplish the essential target of the colonial powers is continuously developing. Finally these powers have transferred their roles to the two contemporary new powers, the United States and the Soviet Union, who have assumed and continue the role with more and better technological means. (For more detail on this subject, *consult* Zallūm, 1961; Ḥusayn, 1954; Demaris, 1974; Bailey, 1942; Smith, 1979.)

The concept of nationalism was originally crystallized by the Islamic Holy Constitution to fuse all contingent and divergent ethnic groups existing into one sociopolitical system for the world. The main factors that have been considered the essential elements of Islamic nationality have been carefully designated by the Islamic Holy Constituion.

1. The language, which contains a tremendous vocabulary that can be developed to meet any challenge of change and development, is deliberately chosen.
2. The common dogmatic belief is united in one entity which all believers must submit to as the supreme Sovereign of the Universe.
3. Finally, common historical tradition is twofold: the historical events which represent most of the civilized world before Islam, including the story of the first human being, Adam; the historical events which escorted the message of Islam as one of the most reliable historical accounts conveyed to us in terms of writing by eyewitnesses who recorded them.

The believers of Islam according to the Islamic Holy Constitution should identify themselves only as Muslim, which is the only citizenship to which they must be affiliated.

The word 'Muslim', used in the Islamic Holy Constitution to identify the believers of God, has been the attribution of such believers even before the last Islamic message existed. All prophets mentioned in the Holy Qur'ān and their followers, including Jews and Christians, were dubbed Muslims (muslimūn). The following Qur'ānic verse of the Islamic Holy Constitution declares that fact and emphasizes that 'Muslim' is the identity which God Himself attributed to those who submit to Him alone since the revelation started.

> And exert yourself in the cause of God with ultimate conceivable effort, He has appointed you and will never deceive you by means of religion [Islam]—the tenet of your Father Abraham. He [God]] has named you Muslims (al-Muslimūn) in this message as He named His worshippers long ago.
>
> *The Qur'ān* 22:78

So it is God who has named the followers of His path 'Muslims' even before the last Islamic message was revealed. The Islamic State must attribute all its citizens to Islam as the only identity which distinguishes them forever from all nations.

The Non-Muslim in the Islamic State

The previous section has emphasized that Islamic citizenship is not to be conferred upon anybody other than a Muslim. It is a political identity for those who apply the system of Islam in their lives. Thus, in conformity with the Islamic Holy Constitution, mankind has been considered either Muslim or non-Muslim. This categorization is merely aimed to distinguish the Muslims with regard to their responsibilities and requirements in the Islamic system, without any intention to discriminate between Muslim and non-Muslim in any other respect, such as humanity, race or colour. The following Qur'ānic verses have asserted this meaning.

> He [God] is Who created you, hence, part of you are disbelievers, and part of you are believers. And God is certainly aware of what you are doing.
>
> *The Qur'ān* 64:2

> Those who disbelieve and turn away from the path of God, their deeds and efforts will be in vain. And those who believe, do righteous deeds and believe in what is revealed to Muḥammad, which is the actual reality from their God, their misdeeds will cease and their worry will be eliminated.
>
> *The Qur'ān* 47:1–2

The verses categorize mankind as believers and disbelievers as a consequence of the acceptance and application of the Islamic system which has to be carried out by the believers, who in turn are rewarded for fulfilling the requirements.

By reviewing the instructions of the Islamic Holy Constitution concerning non-Muslims, it has been found that non-Muslims are classified in three distinct categories with respect to the responsibilities of the Islamic State towards them.

1. Non-Muslims who happen to live within the territory of the Islamic State or in an area controlled by the Islamic State.
2. Non-Muslims who enter the jurisdiction of the Islamic State as merchants, traders, regular visitors and students.
3. Non-Muslims who live outside the territorial jurisdiction of the Islamic State.

This section will confine itself to the first and second categories. The third will be discussed in Chapter 4 with the conceptual framework of peace and war in the Islamic system.

Non-Muslims who live within the territory of the Islamic State, have been conferred special status by the Islamic Holy Constitution. The Declaration of Medina regulates most situations relating to non-Muslims, as in the following verse:

> And the Jews of Banū ʿAwf shall be considered a community (ummah)—themselves and their partisans along with the nation of the believers. For the Jews their religion and for the believers their religion, with the exception that anyone of the Jews who commits a heinous crime or sin will be liquidating himself and his family.
>
> *Declaration of Medina*, verse 26

The above quoted verse specifies by name one single tribe of the Jews and their partisans who were living in Medina at the time—the Jews of Banū ʿAwf. The following eight verses of the Declaration of Medina name other tribes and branches of tribes with their partisans who also have been given the same status as those of Banū ʿAwf. These verses announce that the non-Muslim community or individuals who live within the territory of the Islamic State or want to live within it shall be given permanent resident status, but shall never be considered citizens of the Islamic State unless they profess Islam by their own freewill and after knowing all necessary regulations and commitments, including the law of treason, or the law of apostasy as it has been called.

The basic regulations governing the non-Muslim who has been granted the right of permanent residence by the Islamic Holy Constitution can be summed up in the following articles which are mostly included in the Declaration of Medina (*see* Appendix).

1. They shall be protected by the Islamic State from any outside or inside ignominious acts or attacks. However, in case of outside attack against them, the Islamic State may recruit those who are able to fight with the regular army but never as front ranks in combat troops.
2. They are exempted from military conscription unless they want to enlist, in which case the Islamic State has to enroll them in any unit which does not affect the security of the State for the same period required for citizens.
3. They shall not be allowed to have a permanent position in any of these army units in which they are enrolled unless the Islamic State enacts a special law stipulating its need for them in such positions.
4. In case of their enlistment or their permanent position in the unit, they shall be exempted from paying the required income tax for the period they serve.
5. They are not allowed to work in any public office unless the Islamic State enacts a special law determining their recruitment for such a position, stipulating that holding such office does not affect the security of the Islamic State.
6. The Islamic State shall enact the necessary law to determine the type of professions in which they shall be allowed.
7. Male, non-Muslim, permanent residents who are between the ages of twenty-one and sixty and are fully able to work, shall pay an annual income tax (jizyah) which shall be determined by the Islamic State's enacted law, and which shall not exceed one to five percent of their total annual income.
8. The Islamic State is fully responsible for providing a living for the non-Muslim, permanent resident who cannot work or cannot find a decent job.
9. They have to use the Islamic Court in all their legal cases. However, the Islamic Court shall provide them with a permanent, respectable expert for the cases involving their creed and personal statute, under full supervision of the Islamic Court.

10. They have the full right to leave temporarily or permanently at any time unless their departure affects the security of the Islamic State.
11. All travel rules and requirements designed for the Islamic State's citizens, such as the necessity of documentation and permission, shall be applied to them.
12. Their children must enter the Islamic State educational institutions for elementary and high school diplomas. Their higher education shall be oriented by the Islamic State towards their allowable professions only.
13. They are not allowed to open their own educational institutions; however, their creed shall be taught in their temples under full supervision of the Islamic Court.
14. The *kharāj* system, which is designed for agrarian land owned by non-Muslims, shall be different from tax (zakāh) systems for agrarian land owned by Muslims (both systems will be discussed in Chapter 6).
15. All other regulations and laws not concerning religious duties, applied to the Islamic State's citizens, shall be tacitly applied to all permanent residents.

Non-Muslims who enter the Islamic State as merchants, traders, students, visitors, or Muslims who are not living in the Islamic State, shall be considered aliens and treated accordingly. The Islamic State must enact laws to determine the entrance of aliens into its territory, for any purposes, in accordance with its security requirements. However, diplomats and irregular visitors have to be treated according to international customs and norms.

The non-Muslims who live in the Islamic State's territory have never been considered citizens of the Islamic State. Their status is determined by the Islamic Holy Constitution as permanent or temporary residents who have a special responsibility towards the Islamic State as it does to them. Above all, the Islamic State has to be very careful in the matter of enacting any law concerning those permanent residents, especially in regard to human rights regulations in Islam. However, any of those permanent or temporary residents who at any time professes Islam immediately becomes a citizen and gains the rights and privileges of any other citizen of the Islamic State without any consideration of colour, race or birth place.

Finally, the Islamic Holy Constitution has emphasized certain ground work, such as justice and equality, that is essential in the implementation of the system. Islam, in fact, is the first system in the world to identify Muslims with a certain nationality. It provides the Islamic community with more accurate factors which are necessary for its adherence. Also, Islam has instituted the basic regulation in the treatment of alien or non-Muslim society within or without the Islamic State and confers status on those who live within the territorial jurisdiction of the Islamic State.

3

The Functions and Organization of the Islamic State

Scholars have tried with various theoretical approaches to describe the pattern of the first Islamic State founded by the Prophet of Islam and his four Right-guided successors. Some have argued that it is a theocracy (Wellhausen, 1927, pp. 5–8), a state 'governed by a god or gods' (Smith, 1924, Vol. XII, pp. 287–9). Others have suggested that the Islamic State is monarchical or oligarchical with the authority entrusted by force or reason to one or the few (Kern, 1939, pp. 27–34; Arnold, 1935, pp. 4–37). and still others have deemed that the Islamic state is a universal nomocracy (Arnold, 1935, pp. 4-7), a system of government based on a legal code.

In actuality, none of these terms can be applied to the Islamic State. It is well known that the Prophet of Islam died without providing for an immediate succession. However, in his final days the Prophet ordered Abū Bakr to lead the public prayers (Al-Ṭabarī, 1962, Vol. 3, pp. 196–8), which might have been an indication for Muslims at the time to nominate Abū Bakr as the Prophet's successor. However, after the debate between the representatives of the *Anṣār* and the *Muhājrīn*, Saʿd and Abū Bakr, respectively, in Saqīfat banī Saʿidah (a place in Medina where the debate was held), the election of Abū Bakr has obviously introduced for the first time in world history the 'popular' factor in the selection of the chief executive of the state. To describe the election the Islamic Holy Constitution uses the word *shūrā* or the right of Muslims to participate in the choice of their leader. The introduction and practice of the popular factor in such a selection, as ordered by the Islamic Holy Constitution, means that the ultimate power is seen to flow from, and by the consent of the Muslim Nation. Thus, it is the Islamic democracy which firmly fulfils the dream of human beings as defined in an Aristotelian sense.

However, the Islamic State, by this consideration, is not merely a secular democratic state, as it is certainly not a purely religious one. It is, indeed, the democracy of Islam, the fundamental dual and unique responsibility which incorporates the temporal and spiritual vocations and operation. Its dispensative character promotes and applies, in its full capacity, the instructions of the Islamic Holy Constitution, internally as well as externally. Its laic character fulfils the role of 'Midmost Nation' by perpetuating justice, freedom and equality among mankind. In addition, its ultimate end is to provide all possible means of good and honourable living for human beings, especially those who accept Islam—a preparation for the luxurious life of the next world.

This chapter provides a discussion of two main topics concerning state functions and organizational structures. The first covers the purpose of the Islamic State, its function and services. The second explores the suffrage right, election, and the concept of *bayʿah* in Islam. In addition, we shall discuss the Islamic State's governmental organizations, the legislature, the judiciary and the executive branches. The main focus will be to show who are involved in these areas and how the structures work.

The Purpose of the Islamic State

The primary purposes of the Islamic State are the ensurance of freedom from outside invasions, the security of domestic tranquillity and the provision of justice, equality and personal security for its people. These goals are the major concern and subject of the Declaration of Medina (*see* Appendix, verses 15–19, 32–45). The Declaration of Medina concentrates on these points because the attainment of all other purposes and functions depends on the success of the state in securing the highest degree of order, consistent with the liberty of individuals and groups in Islamic society.

Of course, the application of the Islamic Holy Constitution, the promotion of individual interests and the general welfare of Muslims are among the primary and significant issues with which the Islamic State has to deal. The full application of the Islamic Holy Constitution has attempted to expose the Islamic Nation to one standard of morality, one code of behaviour, one code of religion and one political system. The major aim is to fuse all existing divergences into one homogeneous nation. The goal is to develop individual and public capacities, spiritually and materialistically, as well as to encourage a pragmatic life in this world and in the hereafter. The promotion of an individual's interests and public welfare is emphasized in the following Qur'ānic verse, which argues that a Muslim must devote himself to the next life without ignoring his interests in this world.

> And seek, in whatever God has bestowed upon you, the next world, but do not forget your participation and share in this world, and be nice as God has been kind to you, and never seek doing corruption in the earth. Verily God does not love the corruptors.
>
> *The Qur'ān* 28:77

The Muslim has no right to force himself to extremes of purely spiritual or purely material interests. He has to balance his life among these two concepts. The role of the Islamic state is, then, to provide individuals with the most favourable conditions, consistent with the interests of society as a whole, under which they may complete, develop and fulfil both their roles, their personalities as *mu'minin* (believers) and their responsibilities as human beings. Among these conditions are the protection of personal rights and the effective participation in socio-political activities.

In terms of general or public welfare, the development of public capacities involves care for the common interests of society and provision for united action in achieving goals which individuals and/or associations cannot achieve by themselves alone. Moreover, the Islamic state may suggest the reconciliation of interests among groups and between individuals or groups and the society as a whole.

Finally, it is not the intention of the Islamic State, as a powerful political body, to play any political or social roles in directing the attention of its subjects, or manipulating them, toward specific policies in order to facilitate the politicians' dominant function. The Islamic State's main objective is to apply and enforce Islamic Law which is fully accepted by its citizens, who give their ultimate consent to their leader to exercise the terms and the provisions of the Islamic Holy Constitution over them.

The Function of the Islamic State

The function of the state may be defined in terms of the particular activities in which it engages. In Islam the paramount function of the

Islamic State is to equalize the deployment and diffusion of justice and freedom of belief, or thought, among mankind. The Islamic State government and society are always fully responsible toward those who are tyrannized by their own rulers and who are exposed forcefully and without their express consent to a certain thought or creed. The Islamic State is responsible for emancipating man and allowing him freely to decide upon his own belief and practice. This responsibility is articulated in the following Qurʾānic verses:

> The track [to fight and/or oppress] is open only against those who tyrannize mankind and unlawfully commit outrages in the earth, those shall have a painful chastisement.
>
> *The Qurʾān* 42:42

> Thus, We [God] have rendered you a midmost nation for the purpose of being witnesses upon mankind as the Prophet is being a witness upon you . . .
>
> *The Qurʾān* 2:143

According to the first verse, Muslims bear firmly the responsibility of fighting those who are iniquitous, who enforce their own thought and creed upon other people. The second verse also states this sort of responsibility for Muslims, who have been appointed to be in the middle of the road, between two extremes, not purely religious, nor purely secular. So, being in the very centre Muslims must not be forced by either extremes. The main requirement of such evidence is to participate physically in liberating mankind from any compulsive ideology. Thus, the Islamic State is entitled by the Islamic Holy Constitution to introduce freedom to those who have been oppressed and to let them freely decide their own destiny in regard to their ideological thought.

Of course, other essential functions are necessary to safeguard the state's existence. Most of those functions have been decided and practised by the Prophet and/or his first four Right-guided successors within the foundation of the first state of Islam (Al-Kattānī, n.d., especially Vol. 1, pp. 63–464). These essential functions include the maintenance of an armed force for defence against foreign invasion or domestic violence, as well as the opposition of tyrannies around the world; police forces, for the suppression of crimes and the prosecution of criminals; courts, for the protection of the rights of the individual, the settlement of controversies by legal means, and for the punishment of criminal offenses; foreign service, for the conduct of relations with other states; and, tax collecting and record keeping systems, for the implementation of other functions and ends.

The service functions of the Islamic State include many activities conducive to the attainment of the general welfare of its citizens. One of these services is significantly important and was created by the first Islamic State. This function was certainly unknown before the existence of that first state, i.e., the complete responsibility of the Islamic State to provide at least the very basic means of existence for its citizens or its permanent residents who are either not able to work for any reasonable purpose or who can not find appropriate jobs. The main objective of this responsibility is twofold: humanely, to care for those who are not able to earn their living, and legally, to avoid any criminal act which might be considered by those unable to provide for their own living. This responsibility is one of the most significant purposes for the financial instructions of the Islamic Holy Constitution. The following verses from the Holy Qur'ān and Sunnah, respectively, are demonstrative of the responsibility of such a service:

> Take [an order to the Prophet as the head of the Islamic State] from their wealth [certain percentage as tax] *zakāh* which purifies them and makes their wealth grow.
>
> *The Qur'ān* 9:103

> I am [the Prophet as the head of the Islamic State] responsible for those who do not find a way to be responsible for themselves.
>
> Ibn Ḥanbal, Vol.4, p. 144

The Qur'ānic verse above indicates an explicit order for the state to collect a certain percentage of tax from the rich. The Islamic Holy Constitution calls this tax *zakāh*, which literally means growth. The reward of the zakāh is assured by God in terms of personal purification and continuous growth of wealth. One of the main purposes of the zakāh is to help those who are unable to maintain a certain fixed income.

The verse from the Sunnah attaches the responsibility to the state which is fully accountable for the people in question. On the other hand the Islamic Holy Constitution has warned the believers not to depend entirely on the state responsibility for living, as long as it is possible for them to work and earn their own living. The following verses of the Sunnah emphasize that meaning:

He who asks people to increase his wealth, is asking for a live coal, so he may decrease it or increase it.

Muslim, *Zakāh*, 105

It is best for a person to go and get some firewood on his back and sell it than to ask people who either give to him or refuse him because the upper hand is much better than the lower one.

Muslim, *Zakāh*, 106

Thus, the Islamic State's responsibility does not confine itself to governing socio-political affairs, but it must go beyond this to concern itself with and care for every individual interest in the Islamic Nation.

Other obligatory service functions, such as the building of hospitals, libraries, schools, railways and highways, are charged as well to be the responsibility of the Islamic State, which should allocate funds for public services in its annual budget.

THE BUSINESS FUNCTION

The Islamic State should involve itself in the sort of business for which private capital is not available, or if available, in insufficient amounts. The state may also become involved in enterprises with inadequate services or in which excessive charges are levied by private concerns. Services such as transportation, telecommunications may also be carried out by the Islamic State. However, when private enterprises are ready to take over these services at the same or lower charges, the Islamic State may cease its involvement unless the role of the state is necessary for the welfare of the people who depend on the state. The Islamic State must pass laws to determine the maximum profit of private enterprises, to create competition among them. Finally, it is the Islamic State's responsibility to determine, by law, the minimum wages and labourers and professionals. The state must also regulate, instruct and standardize all professional services and the production of goods, either locally made or imported, to protect consumers. Sometimes the Islamic State has to subsidize some of the essential commodities for the public good.

The Organization of the Islamic State

THE RIGHTS AND DUTIES OF THE ISLAMIC NATION

There is no doubt that the Islamic Nation influences greatly the political activities of the state. The Islamic Holy Constitution has granted certain powers to the Islamic Nation to participate in its political and social institutions, articulated in the Islamic Holy Constitution by the Arabic word *shūrā*, or the right to participate in choosing the leader of the Islamic State and in any decision that is not covered by the Islamic Holy Constitution. However, the Islamic Nation has, in return, been commissioned by the Islamic Holy Constitution with certain duties that have to be carried out by all Muslims. These political rights and duties are: 'shūrā', election, 'bayʿah' and obedience.

Shūrā, or suffrage, is a privilege granted by the Islamic Holy Constitution to an expressly designated group of the Islamic Nation, entitling them to participate in the choice of their leadership. Any decisions that are not covered by the Islamic Holy Constitution, especially those concerning their destiny, may be questioned by them. The Islamic Holy Constitution has enfranchised each individual citizen in the Islamic State, male or female, who has reached the age of discretion, the legal age between nine and twenty-five when the Muslim is required to perform religious duties. The Islamic Nation may decide the age of enfranchisement, which is normally between eighteen and twenty-one, with twenty-one being the favoured age. Such power has been articulated in the following verse:

> And those who respond to their God, perform the prayers, their ruling system is based on the right of *shūrā* amongst them [that is either by consensus or election], and from what We have provided them they outlay [to the poor].
>
> *The Qurʾān* 42:38

This verse, quoted in the previous chapter in the discussion of sovereignty, describes some of the believers' characteristics. Among these is the full, indispensable right of the Islamic Nation to participate in the selection of those who will be responsible for running its affairs and applying the Islamic Holy Constitution.

Shūrā, the word used in the Arabic version of the verse, is a discussion held by a group of people in order to reach a firm decision in any matter. It can also be an alternative resolution for a person who seeks an opinion concerning a certain problem. Of the alternatives provided, he shall then choose one as a solution (Ibn Manzūr, n.d., s.v. *shawara*). The Islamic Holy Constitution has drawn, in one word, the major principle of suffrage—the right of the believers to choose their leadership from among themselves by a complete concensus, or by an absolute majority, as the nature of the meaning the shūrā has dictated.

Thus, the Islamic Holy Constitution firmly emphasizes the right of Muslims to discuss and choose in such important matters as the leadership of the Islamic Nation. At the same time, the Islamic Holy Constitution abstains from setting down the methods of conducting this right: although the instructions might have been perfect for the time the Islamic message was revealed, they would most probably not have been suitable for the future.

Election is one of the phases of shūrā when concensus is hard to reach. After the death of the Prophet of Islam, the opinion was that an electorate, if left to itself, could not make the best choice among candidates, especially with the complete lack of any immediate communication with other parts of the state (Ibn Hishām, 1955, Vol. 2, p. 656; Al-Ṭabarī, 1962, Vol. 3, p. 203ff). For this reason, the election was confined to an intermediate group of able and responsible persons of the capital of the State—Medina (Al-Ṭabari, 1962, Vol. 3, p. 204; Al-Bukhārī, 1961, *Muhāribīn*, 17). The group was dubbed by Islamic jurists *Ahl al-Ḥal wa al-ʿAqd* (Al-Māwardī, 1966, pp. 5–8). At the time of the Right-guided Caliphs, leaders were inaugurated after certain shūrā procedures which confirmed the principles of the right of choice and discussion. No scholar can assert that their take over as leaders of the first Islamic Nation was done by means of force.

It was after his famous debate in the meeting of Saqīfat banī Saʿidah that Abū Bakr nominated two persons for the high office in the state (ʿUmar and Abū ʿUbaydah), and asked the meeting to choose one of them (Al-*Ṭabarī, 1962, Vol. 3, p.* 206). However, ʿUmar hated to be a leader of the Muslims while Abū Bakr was one of them; ʿUmar interrupted the silence, saying: 'Is there any one of you who can stand to be a leader before the feet which the Prophet was forwarding in our prayers' (Al-Ṭabarī, 1962, Vol. 3, p. 202). ʿUmar reminded the meeting that the Prophet had chosen the most qualified man to be his deputy in leading the prayer and had even prayed behind him. ʿUmar pointed out that as long as the Prophet chose Abū Bakr to lead in the most important religious duty, why should the believers hesitate to appoint him leader of their non religious affairs. ʿUmar immediately put out his hand and made the oath of commitment, *bayʿah*, acknowledging Abū Bakr as the leader of the Islamic Nation after the Prophet. So, the meeting followed ʿUmar making bayʿah with a very few exceptions (Al-Ṭabarī, 1962, Vol. 3, pp. 206–209).

The succession of ʿUmar is another model of the practice of shūrā dictated by prevailing circumstances. Close to his death, Abū Bakr addressed the Muslims of Medina, saying, 'Have you agreed on the one I have concluded to be your leader after me? I swear by God I have scrutinized all possible alternatives and I do not choose a relative of mine. I have chosen ʿUmar ibn al-Khaṭṭāb as your leader after me. Are you hearing and are you obeying?' The gathered Muslims immediately answered 'Yes, we are' (Al-Ṭabarī, 1962, Vol. 3, p. 428). Al-Ṭabari and other historians affirmed that Abū Bakr had discussed ʿUmar's succession with an intermediate group such as Abd al-Rḥaman ibn ʿAwf and ʿUthām ibn ʿAffān, who confirmed Abū Bakr's choice (Al-Ṭabarī, 1962, Vol. 3, p. 428).

One absolute fact stands out: the respective succession after the Prophet's death of the four Right-guided Caliphs as the leaders of the Islamic Nation did not take place forcibly nor inherently. They were elected in confortmity with prevailing circumstances. Rationally, it is impossible to expect people living around the middle of the seventh century A.D. to hold an election of equal standard to those held today. The decision was made by a group of respected, able and responsible Muslims who, after much discussion, nominated or agreed upon a leader to run the affairs of the state and asked the populace to perform bayʿah to him.

It should be remembered that whatever methods were used in the past they should not be held by Muslims as precedents that have to be strictly followed as provisions of the Islamic Holy Constitution. It is not meant that following the precedents of these Right-guided Caliphs is wrong, but that in similar situations Muslims must not blindly follow any precedent before examining all the circumstances and comparing them to the precedents. The elections of the four Right-guided Caliphs were carried out according to circumstances prevailing at the time. Today, with advanced technology and world-wide communications, Muslims must not imitate actions and methods of fourteen centuries ago that were used more because modern communication was not available than because God had so ordered it.

The Islamic Holy Constitution gives the Islamic Nation the right to choose people who can carry out and enforce the law of God and with whose standards they are satisfied. This right was practised by the first generation of the Islamic Nation in accordance with their times. The Islamic Holy Constitution does not restrict Muslims to certain methods, but gives them full freedom to select the technique which fulfils their ultimate desire to invoke justice and equality through the use of shūrā in electing their own leaders. What are the most desirable methods to be implemented now by the Islamic Nation to elect their leaders. Which methods are compatible with the provisions of the Islamic Holy Constitution in general? Below are the suggested major steps in the election of the public officers of the Islamic State. These steps supposedly do not instigate disputes concerning the provisions of the Islamic Holy Constitution. They were chosen after a complete review of the general and specific provisions of the Islamic Holy Constitution. Moreover, almost all regulations, rules and procedures of direct and indirect elections which are exercised in democratic and non-democratic countries have been reviewed.

An election, according to modern political definition, is a choice by persons qualified to vote, among candidates for public office (Phillips, 1975, p. 5–6; Rietman, 1972, p. 3–6). The major elements of any election are the electorate and those to be elected. Other elements involved can include the number of officers to be chosen, the frequency of elections, the secrecy of voting and the administrative procedures for conducting the elections.

1. The *electorate* in the Islamic State consists of all citizens, male and female, who, at the day of election, are twenty-one years of age. The Islamic Holy Constitution does not indicate any differentiation between male and female in this right. On the contrary, it was reported in the records of the Sunnah that the Prophet had received the commitment oath from women too (*see* Muslim, *Īmārah:* 88; the *Holy Qur'ān* 60:12). Furthermore, the following Qur'ān verse emphasizes this general equality: 'The believers are but brothers . . .' (*The Qur'ān* 49:10).

2. *Public officers* who are to be elected, ranking from members of the Islamic Congress up to the president of the Islamic State, have to meet certain general and specific criteria. The specific rules of the election will be discussed under each type of public office. A public officer must either be a citizen of the Islamic State by birth, or if not a descendant of Muslims must have had citizenship at least ten years prior to the election. This last provision is merely to guard against those who claim to be Muslims for certain purposes. A public officer must also have obtained an academic degree from a recognizeable institution in any

discipline and must have worked as a professional for at least five years. He must be fully sound in body and mind. (Those who are physically handicapped but with total use of their mind and sight shall be exempted from this requirement.) And a public officer must never have been convicted of treason, bribery or other high crimes or misdemeanors.

3. *Nominations* for public office. No political parties will be allowed in the Islamic State because all Muslims embrace one doctrine and acknowledge one ideological system, Islam. This prevents any individual from nominating himself or asking to be appointed in any official position. The reason for not accepting self-nomination is that public offices in the Islamic State are great burdens which will be accounted for by God in addition to personal deeds. They are absolutely not honorary social ranks or a means to make fortunes, as asserted by the following Sunnah verses:

> Abū Mūsā, one of the Prophet Companions, said: 'I entered the Prophet's house with two men of my clan: both of them asked the Prophet, saying: "O Messenger of God, would you please appoint us in one of these public offices which God has put in your hands?' The Prophet said: "We, by God's name, do not appoint to the public offices [in our state] those who ask for them, nor any one who is covetous for such a thing".'
>
> Muslim, *Īmārah*, 14

> Abū Dharr said to the Prophet: 'O Messenger of God, do you intend to assign me to one of these public offices?' The Prophet puts his hand on my shoulder saying: 'O Abū Dharr you are such a delicate person, and authority is a trust as it will be a cause of humiliating regretfulness on Resurrection Day, but not for those who fulfill its obligation, and properly give the duties required thereon'.
>
> Muslim, *Īmārah*, 16

> Maʿqil said: I heard the Prophet say: 'Any one who becomes responsible, by God ordained [holding such public office] and he cheats therein until his death. God has forbidden him to enter paradise'.
>
> Muslim, *Īmārah*, 21

> ʿAbd al-Rahmān ibn Samurah said: The Prophet told me: 'O ʿAbd al-Raḥmān, do not ask for public office, because if it has been given

to you accordingly, you will be left to depend on yourself; but if you have been assigned to such an office without requesting it, you will be backed on this appointment by God'.

Muslim, *Īmārah*, 13

4. *Election procedures.* Election for public offices in the Islamic State shall be carried out, directed and supervised by the Islamic State Supreme Court. The Court shall provide and arrange all requirements for election, such as times, pamphlets and ballots. Since the Islamic State does not exist now and there is no Islamic Supreme Court, Muslims in all Islamic lands have to choose a temporary Constituent Assembly. This assembly shall consist of ninety-nine permanent jurists and professionals in different fields of knowledge who are widely known by the Muslim electorate as Islamicists. These people shall supervise and conduct the first election of the Islamic State as *Ahl al-Ḥal wa-al-ʿAqd.* After the election, the Islamic State Supreme Court must have full and complete information regarding the financial situation of individuals elected for public office. Throughout their terms of service, the Supreme Court shall regularly supervise their financial situation and enterprises. One of the main purposes of this provision is to assure that the power of public offices is not misused. The following verse of the Prophet's Sunnah explains and warns such misusers of power.

The Prophet had appointed a man from the Azd tribe (his nickname was Ibn al-Lutabiyyah) in one of these public offices to collect taxes, zakāh. When he came back from his mission, the Prophet asked him to submit his bookkeeping to the public treasury. He set a part of what he collected aside saying 'those are for the public treasury and those have been given to me as a gift'. The Prophet angrily responded saying: 'You had better stay in your father's house and wait for people to give you a gift'. The Prophet, then, stood up on his pulpit addressing the people, saying after praising God: 'What has happened to those men whom I appointed to such public services to which I have been entrusted, when they return to render their accountings saying: "this part has been given to me as a gift". Why do they not remain in their own house and wait for someone to present them with a gift. By Him in whose hand is my soul, any one of you who gets or conceals anything of what he has been entrusted, even a small needle, shall be severely taken to account on

Resurrection Day'. The Prophet then raised his hand up and said: 'O, God I have conveyed'.

Muslim, *Īmārah*, 26

According to this writer's knowledge, this is the first legal act executed in such a manner. Any gift to public officers must be prohibited and if taken, it should be submitted to the public treasury. Public officers must be questioned about their own wealth before and after holding office. As a general rule, any kind of gift presented to any state official shall immediately enter the public treasury, without exception. These are the general rules of electing the Islamic State officers. (Other specific rules will be presented later for the three main branches of administration.)

Bayʿah and obedience are the logical consequence, of having the right of suffrage. The Islamic Holy Constitution has imposed two sorts of obligations which have to be completely fulfilled by each individual citizen in the Islamic State. The first of these obligatory tasks is the bayʿah, or the Commitment Oath. It is recommended that every individual citizen who has the right of franchise take such an oath, confirmed in the following Sunnah verse:

Whosoever dies without having bound himself with *Bayʿah* [Commitment Oath] will die as in the death of Jāhilīyyah [that is the death will not be in the terms of Islam].

Muslim, *Īmārah*, 58

The Commitment Oath is an acknowledgement by the Muslim individual of his complete satisfaction in using his right to choose and vote for the Islamic State administration. It is also a commitment to exert himself as a citizen of the Islamic State and to participate in carrying out the Islamic Holy Constitution. The Commitment Oath should consist of the following statement:

By God's name, I (...) will be, myself and my wealth at the disposal of the Islamic State represented by the head of the state (...) in terms of good and bad conditions with appropriate courtesy as long as the administration is following and applying the Islamic Holy Constitution. Thereupon, I will, by all means, help, advise, participate, and obey the administration in any order issued by the

> head of the Islamic State or his officers without delay or repudiation, as much as I can do so.
>
> Muslim, *Īmārah*, 31–58

One of the most significant objectives of such a commitment is to affirm the stability and cohesion of the Islamic Nation. This bayʿah is a commitment to God Himself such that the individual will be one of those who acknowledge His sovereignty and apply His law on earth:

> Verily, those who commit themselves to you [the Prophet], they assuredly are committing themselves to God. God's Hand is over their hand. Thereupon, whosoever infringes, indeed, his infringement will be on his part alone; and whosoever remains in his covenant to God, He will bestow on him immense reward.
>
> *The Quarʾān*, 48:10

Even though this verse was addressing the Prophet of Islam and describing an existing situation, it is not restricted to the occasion which prevailed at the time. It actually supports the Sunnah verse quoted above. Bayʿah should not be considered a commitment to the head of the state as a person, but, in more general terms, it is a renewal each time of the covenant of God and the submission to Him alone. It is a symbolic reminder for Muslims that they are continuously bound to the Shahādah, the confirmation of entering Islam. For this reason the Sunnah makes bayʿah equal to the Shahādah (Muslim, *Īmārah*, 58).

As a consequence of bayʿah, the Islamic Holy Constitution has plainly ordered Muslims to obey fully those whom they have chosen to be their leaders:

> O, you who believe, obey God and obey the Prophet and those who are in power amongst you. Thereupon, if you have any matter of dispute, refer it to God and to the Prophet [that is, the Islamic Holy Constitution] if you certainly believe in God and the Last Day, that is the best deed and it is better to interpret.
>
> *The Qurʾān* 4:59

Thus, Obedience is the final phase of shūrā. Once Muslims have the right to discuss, choose and commit themselves, they have to obey their leaders. In doing so, they will obey their Holy Constitution. The verse above ends with the assertion that any dispute between the ruler and the ruled should be settled by reference to their Islamic Holy Constitution.

Finally, the Islamic Holy Constitution has introduced the right of people to choose their own ruling system, and, in turn, to elect their own representatives who will run their social and political affairs. The Islamic democracy was practised for the first and last time by the four Right-guided Caliphs albeit, in a very primitive way. They practised Islamic democracy in conformity to the predicaments of their time; it is difficult to imagine that such people could deal with the problems they had to face.

THE LEGISLATURE

The legislature is the major structure of the Islamic State, the nucleus of all distinguished offices in the governmental order including the presidential office of the Islamic State. From the Prophet's closest advisors and Shūrā Committee, who took precedence, the Prophet appointed governors, political envoys, army leaders and state officers, and the four Right-guided Caliphs were chosen after the Prophet's death (Ibn Hishām, 1955, Vol. 1, p. 620; Al-Kattānī, n.d., Vol. 1, pp. 240, 477–80). The legislature formulated the Constitutional Law (Shariʿāh) in accordance with the Islamic Holy Constitution, as well as the laical will of the Islamic State. It usually exercises a degree of supervision and control over the other branches of the government. The power of the legislature may incorporate four main functions: constituent, electoral, law-making and supervisory powers.

Constituent Function

The first task of the legislature will be to constitutionalize all areas which are not covered by the Islamic Holy Constitution in detail, especially the governmental order of the Islamic State, its competent authorities and the election procedures. This supplementary constitution can be amended by the Muslim electorate at any time there is an urgent need to do so. It is obvious that the Islamic Holy Constitution cannot be amended by any power in the Islamic State. However, the legislature may propose or discuss a proposal handed to it by the President of the Islamic State to suspend only temporarily one or more of its provisions (not including the Divine Services and personal statute provisions), under any unexpectedly severe conditions. The legislature may also propose to the Islamic State Supreme Court the necessity of restricting enforcement officially to one or more available hermeneutic alternatives in the Constitutional Law, thereby blocking any loopholes which may be exploited by the Islamic Nation (Muslim, 1956, *Ṭalāq*, 15–17).

Electoral Function

In general, voting in constitutional matters must not always be exercised by the legislature. However, any matter brought up in the legislature must be thoroughly studied and discussed and then, the most appropriate alternative to the standard of the Islamic Holy Constitution, which coincides with the interests of the Islamic Nation, should be adopted. The vote is indispensable only when the alternatives are equal. Jurists and professional members of the Islamic Congress will vote by provinces and profession respectively (each province shall have two votes and each profession shall have one vote only). The legislature has the power to nominate candidates for presidential office, vice president, members of the Islamic Supreme Court and provincial governors for direct election by the Muslim electorate. The legislature and other public officers are directly appointed by the electorate after taking the oath of office. The members of the first legislative body and State Supreme Court shall take the oath of office before the constituent assembly, which will then be terminated following the takeover of the State Supreme Court. The legislature may veto any appointment to the cabinet or to presidential advisors who are not nominated from the legislative body, especially in sensitive areas such as foreign and defence offices.

Statute-Making Function

The legislature has the power to create statutes in all areas not covered by the Islamic Holy Constitution. Companions' opinion and famous jurists' views have to be considered only if the existing situation is similar to theirs. However, these new statutes must be confined to the liberal spirit of the Islamic Holy Constitution and conform to its terms of justice and equality. It should be noted here that all such statutes are susceptible to change and development according to circumstances.

Control of Administration

By far the most significant function of the legislature is the supervision of the administration. In addition, the legislature has the power to approve proposals to establish new departments or agencies and to institute regulations to determine their duties and functions. It may also alter or abolish departments or agencies at will. Major treaties, which affect the defence or economy of the Islamic State, have to be ratified before they become effective. The legislature can dispose of an incumbent officer by impeachment. If the individual is not subject to impeachment, it can petition the executive to order the removal of the officer on grounds of unworthiness or by voting lack of confidence. The decision to remove any officer shall be presented to the Islamic Supreme Court for final approval. As a necessary adjunct to the execution of these duties, the Islamic legislature has full power to investigate, to summon witnesses and to compel the presentation of any sort of document which may be required. The results of investigations must be announced by the Islamic Supreme Court to keep the electorate informed of public affairs.

General Discipline

In order that the legislative branch may not be interfered with by the executive, a number of constitutional safeguards shall be provided by the Islamic legislature at its first session. Members of the legislature, while attending sessions or travelling to and from them, may not be arrested except with a clear order signed by the Chief Justice of the Islamic State Supreme Court. They are immune from any charge if their political attitude is against the existing administration, unless their views affect the Islamic Nation's unity, or go against the provisions of the Islamic Holy Constitution. The Islamic Court may interfere in a possible arrest by first warning the individual to restrict his views to the provisions of the Islamic Holy Constitution. If the individual maintains his attitude, the Islamic Supreme Court may issue a resolution eliminating the immunity and summoning him to the court for legal action.

Legislative Structure

The Islamic legislature, *Majlis al-Shūrā al-Islāmī*, or the Islamic Congress, is bicameral, consisting of the House of Jurists, *Majlis al-Fuqahā'*, and the House of Professionals, *Majlis al-Khubarā'*. The main concept behind this dualism is to fulfil one of the major ends for the existence of the Islamic Nation as the 'Midmost Nation', i.e., to combine the secular and the religious positions in one unique character, that is, Islam.

The Islamic concept of a human being is not merely a soul, nor is he an insignificant body endowed with bestial instincts. A human being has both a body and soul and needs certain direction lest one faction gains control over another. While Sufism teaches that the soul is predominant over the material body, the unlimited bestiality exhibited in every corner of the world represents the dominance of materialism. An equilibrium between these two aspects is indispensable. Thus the clever way is to hold the spiritual and the secular aspects in one straight line running in the same direction.

Thus, the most effective branch in the Islamic State should not consist only of a purely religious structure nor a solely secular one. While the Jurists represent religion, the professionals who specialize in different fields of knowledge represent the secular side of government.

The House of Jurists consists of those people who devoted themselves to the study of the Islamic Holy Constitution and who have developed the ability to explicate, extract and extrapolate law out of its texts. Of course, their outstanding knowledge in Islamic language is fundamental, as is their memorization of the Holy Qur'ān and large parts of the records of the Prophet's Sunnah, especially parts concerning instructions.

The House of the Professionals are those who specialize in one type of knowledge gained by studying for years at recognized academic institutions. Professionals also should have memorized the Holy Qur'ān, or at least a large portion, including the regulatory verses. Besides an outstanding knowledge of the Islamic language, they should be well acquainted with the records of the Prophet's Sunnah.

Tenure of Office

The period during which representatives serve in the Islamic Congress may be fixed. Although there is nothing firmly establishing the ideal period, we would suggest a fixed term of eight years for the House of Jurists and seven for the House of Professionals. The members of both houses may be re-elected for two additional terms. The advantage of this provision is that the legislature may continue if it has the confidence of the electorate, or it may be dissolved if public confidence is lacking. The fixed term gives an opportunity to younger people to participate in the legislature.

Base of Representation

In the Islamic State, a member of the legislative assembly speaks and acts on behalf of the entire Muslim Nation, including the special constituents who elected him. His dual responsibility makes representation seem more difficult. He has a responsibility to his constituents to present and look out for their interest in accordance with the provisions of the Islamic Holy Constitution. His second, and probably largest, burden is as a representative of a government office which acts for the Islamic Nation as a whole. Of course, it is agreed by both sides (the constituents and their representative) that the interests of the Islamic Nation, as a whole, must have priority over the interests of any individual or group.

System of Representation

Two distinct systems have been chosen to elect the jurists and professionals. The geographical system may be used to elect the members of House of Jurists, and the functional system to elect the members of the House of Professionals. Under the geographical system the Islamic State will be divided into provinces, containing, under ideal conditions, an equal number of people who will choose two jurists to represent them in the House of Jurists. In the functional system, the Islamic State Supreme Court will enact laws giving each profession existing in the Islamic State its own association. The Court will make certain rules for the associations. The Supreme Court must differentiate between the professional associations and labour guilds, which will also be allowed with certain special rules. Both groups will be under the complete supervision of the Islamic Supreme Court and the Judiciary System.

Nomination and Election of Representatives

THE HOUSE OF JURISTS In regard to the jurists, the Islamic Supreme Court shall publish and distribute nationwide at the beginning of the election year a pamphlet containing the names of well known and legally recognized jurists from all over the Islamic State. Names of those jurists can be arranged under each province alphabetically. The pamphlet may also contain a picture and a biographical sketch and should include a special page for the electorate's use, providing a space for the elector's name and number, his position, city and province and space for him to list the jurists in order of preference. Another special page containing the commitment oath should also be included. (A number might be given to each citizen of the Islamic State at the very first day of enrolment in an institution of learning, i.e., elementary school; this number could be used as a personal identification number throughout a person's lifetime.)

It is not necessary to obtain the jurist's consent to be elected for public offices because such offices are a burden and not a position conferring status. To introduce jurists to the electorate, each has to choose one legislative topic, whether covered by the Islamic Holy Constitution or not, and discuss it nationwide, using the media. These discussions have to be scheduled at least two weeks after the distribution of election pamphlets and must be completed by three months of that date. Immediately after these discussions, the Islamic Supreme Court will fix the election day, allowing the electorate to vote in each province. One week after the election day, at the latest, the Islamic Supreme Court will declare the results. The first two jurists in each province who gained the majority will be the representatives of that province.

THE HOUSE OF PROFESSIONALS In regard to the Professionals the Islamic Court will ask each professional association to nominate at least six of its well known members as candidates for general election and the Islamic Nation will then select two from each profession to be the representatives in their fields. (Jurists' associations have to be represented in this election, too.) The professional's consent is not required for such public offices for the same reason as explained for the jurists. To introduce those professionals to the electorate, each professional also has to choose a topic related to his own profession and discuss it nationwide through the media. These discussion programmes have to be scheduled, at the latest, two weeks after the Islamic Court has announced the names of the professionals and published pictures and biographical sketches of the candidates in a special pamphlet. Directly after the professionals' discussions, the Islamic Supreme Court will determine the election day so the voters can vote to choose their representatives. No later than a week after election day, the Islamic Supreme Court must declare the results. The first two professionals in each discipline who gained the majority will be the representatives of the Islamic Nation in the House of Professionals.

In general, either the election of the jurists or the professionals has to precede the other by at least one month. And by the month of *Shawwāl*, the tenth month of the Islamic lunar calendar, the newly elected congress will take over and prepare for the election of the other branches of government.

The Provincial Congress will be elected in the same manner. The provincial Supreme Court will be responsible for conducting and supervising provincial election procedures. Members of the Provincial Congress, jurists and professionals, may be elected at the time of the State Congress election for the first time. Terms in the Provincial Congress are only for seven years but may be extended by two terms only for both houses.

THE JUDICIARY

In the Islamic State, the liberty and honour of individuals depend upon the fairness of the courts in protecting them from other individuals and from any tyrannical or overzealous governmental officers. Maintaining peace within the state is as much dependent upon the justice with which disputes are settled and prescribed criminal laws are executed as upon the use of force.

The Islamic judiciary system, as presented by the role of the Prophet and his appointed judges (Al-Kattānī, n.d., Vol. 1, pp. 250–64), emphasized the complete separation of the judiciary power from control of legislative and/or executive powers. This separation is considered essential to the preservation of individual dignity and liberty, even though at the beginning, the individual appointees could simultaneously serve as judge and executive because the number of the believers was fewer. However, that did not mean that the judiciary should be under the control of any power. When the Islamic State expanded after the Prophet's death, the leaders of the first Islamic Nation immediately appointed separate individuals for each office. In fact, the judiciary, with its great tasks and responsibility before God and with its non-partisanship, usually attracts less public attention than do the other governmental branches. However, its functions, organization and procedures demand an equal critical understanding.

Function of the Judiciary

The overall function of the judiciary is to apply the law with certainty and uniformity to specific cases. Ordinarily, judges will not act in the absence of a bona fide or actual case *al-sidq*, between parties. When a case is presented, the duty of a court is first to establish the facts and then to discover the law applicable to the case. Sometimes the law is not clear because the statute makers do not always specify the circumstances of each individual case, or because the wording of the statute is more general, or because two or more laws are applicable to the case. The court must resolve these difficulties by determining the exact meaning of the law, expanding its details and applying the general principles of justice. The judge may become the virtual creator of part of the law for the particular case at hand. These ideas can easily be extracted from the following Sunnah verses:

> Verily, you come to me with your legal cases; and probably some of you may present his case more eloquently than the other. For the sake of God I am but a human being, I will judge according to what I hear. Therefore, any one I accordingly give him the legal right of the other. I am giving him an appropriate place in hell, if he wants to take it or leave it.
>
> Al-Bukhārī, *Ahkām*, 20

> 'O, Muᶜādh, which laws are you going to apply in your judgement'? Muᶜādh said, 'I will apply the Qur'ānic Laws'. The Prophet then said, 'What are you doing if you do not find such a law in the Qur'ān?' He said, 'I will apply the Prophet's Sunnah'. The Prophet repeated. 'If you do not find such law in Sunnah!' He said, 'I will try my utmost and judge accordingly'. The prophet pleasantly put his hand on Muᶜādh's chest and said, 'Praise be to God who directs the messenger of the Messenger of God to the correct way which satisfies God and His Prophet'.
>
> Ibn Ḥanbal, Vol. 5, pp. 230, 236, 242

In the first verse the Prophet directed that the presentation of a legal case before the court must be based on a bona fide or an ultimate truth. He warned those who untruthfully presented their legal cases to deceive the judges that they certainly would lead themselves directly to hell fire. In the second verse the Prophet is directing judges to one of the most significant aspects in the judiciary function. He is teaching them that their role in courts is more than hearing disputed parties and finding out the already made law and applying it. Their momentous role is to apply the principle of justice, because the law, in so many cases, is not made to fit exactly to all presented legal cases. Judges have to be the substantial creators of law for the particular cases that come before them. This principle was detailed in the letter of ᶜUmar, the second Right-guided Caliph, to one of his famous judges, Abū Mūsā al-Ashᶜar (Ibn al-Qayyim, 1968, Vol. 1, p. 85–6).

The weight which courts give to previous decisions must be regarded as a precedent for future decisions. This principle is known in the Islamic judiciary system as *Kitāb al-Aqḍiyah*, 'Record of Legal Cases'.

It is also known in Anglo-American jurisprudence as *stare decisis*, to stand by a decision (Abraham, 1980, p. 347; Al-Qurṭubī, 1976; Al-Māwardī, 1966, Vol. 2, pp. 73–8). However, the Islamic Court does not have to stand by, or stick to, any previous decisions with the exception of those made by the Prophet. The Companions' decisions (especially those who were appointed as judges, including the four Right-guided Caliphs), may be considered in similar cases before courts come to a conclusion. The most important advantage of *stare decisis* is to assure uniformity in the application of law. It also gives courts a greater opportunity to revise previous decisions in accordance with any new substantial evidence. Above all, studying and reviewing such decisions by law students gives them a broader conceptual framework for the principles of justice (Al-Māwardī, 1971, Vol. 1, pp. 685–90).

The function of the law is to settle disputes, prevent wrongful acts, encourage good deeds, issue declaratory judgements and judicial reviews, and a host of miscellaneous activities which are less judicial in character but which require the knowledge and authority of a judge. Moreover, the judiciary in the Islamic State is fully responsible for conducting, executing and issuing the necessary election publications for all public officers.

THE SETTLEMENT OF DISPUTES Both civil and criminal cases are brought before the Islamic Court. A civil case, either actions at law or equity suits, is a case between individuals. In deciding it, judges settle claims to property, award damages or take other appropriate actions. A criminal case is brought in the name of the Islamic state against a person accused of a misdemeanor or felony. The court may determine whether a person is innocent or guilty and may invoke the penalty provided by law (Al-Māwardī, 1971, Vol. 2, pp. 330–5).

PREVENTION OF WRONGFUL ACTS By means of writs and restraining orders, a court may act to prevent threatened infractions of the law. In the Islamic state such matters come within the jurisdiction of the Islamic courts. The Islamic Holy Constitution requires Muslims to have a group of people among them to take care of such matters. A Qur'anic verse states:

> Let there be a group from amongst you calling to goodness, ordering equitableness, and warning against reprehensive acts. Those are assuredly the successful.
>
> *The Qur'ān*, 3:104

The best group to prevent threatened infractions of the law is the judicial community because of its specialization in Islamic Law. However, the Islamic Supreme Court can commission any person or group to help in carrying out the Islamic Holy Constitution's order. Its principal writ should indicate an injunction requiring a person to refrain from specific acts which are not to be conducted by Muslims. At the same time, Muslims must be reminded by the judicial community to do good and pleasant deeds that result in the blessing of God. Failure to obey such injunctions constitute contempt of court and may be punished by fine or imprisonment. In order to make such injunctions permanent, a temporary 'blanket injunction' may never be issued in such cases before a complete hearing.

DECLARATORY JUDGEMENTS The Islamic State Supreme Court, in actual controversies, renders declaratory judgement—a judicial determination of the right of professional organizations and guilds existing under the statute, contracts, wills, or other documents. Such judgements, called *Al-Shurūṭ*, enable the parties involved to ascertain their respective rights without becoming involved in wasteful litigation and without having to prove that any wrong has been done or is immediately threatened. Although declaratory judgements do not relieve the parties, they are binding on the participants.

JUDICIAL REVIEW The basis for the Islamic doctrine of judicial review was laid down by a group of the Companions in the famous case of ʿUmar versus the fighters. Judicial review means, in effect, that the Islamic State Supreme Court and Provincial Supreme Courts, as ultimate legal authorities, must compare a statute with the Islamic Holy Constitution. If they find a conflict or find that the legislature lacked power to make a statute, the courts must resolve the conflict in favor of the Constitution because it is the Supreme Law of the land. In the Islamic State, there is no such thing as an unconstitutional law, for such a statute could never have had legal existence. The same rule is applied when acts of executive officers are in question. The decision of the Islamic State Supreme Court as to the meaning of the Islamic Holy Constitution is final in a particular case, though in later cases the court may find reasons for refusing to follow the precedent.

REVIEW OF EXECUTIVE ACTS The Islamic State Supreme Court exercises its power of judicial review over all acts issued by the executive, even when suits have been brought against the head of the Islamic State as an individual. It has to interfere when the head of the Islamic State unconstitutionally proclaims that certain territories belong to the Islamic State or when he has intervened with armed forces to support or suppress disorders within foreign states. The Court also has the power to declare such treaties unconstitutional. It may uphold or reject those acts of cabinet officers which have been committed under presidential direction. It can hold officials of the executive department to strict legal accountability for their public acts, as it can issue *writs of mandamus*, ordering officials to perform duties clearly prescribed by law. The Islamic State Supreme Court is the only power which has the right to issue a declaratory writ to discharge, impeach, or imprison any public officer, executive, or legislator.

REVIEW OF LEGISLATION The Islamic Supreme Court has the power to review all types of statutes issued by the legislature in their final form and before their declaration as a law. The Islamic Congress can declare the legality of a statute after fifteen working days from submitting it to the court if the court fails to indicate officially its unconstitutionality within that period.

Organization of the Judiciary

In establishing a judiciary, the goal is to create a court structure that will be convenient for litigants and that will be expert and certain in its application of the law. Convenience is attained by a territorial distribution of courts. Expertness is attained through specialized courts, such as those that hear only civil, criminal, commercial or equity cases. Certainty is attained through the establishment of appellate courts to review the decisions of the lower courts and to correct their errors.

Structure of the Court System

The judiciary structure is always subject to change and development according to circumstances. The necessity of appointing judges is a precedent of the act of the Prophet and his successors, with respect to the needs of the Muslim societies. The Islamic State Supreme Court, with the advice and co-operation of the legislative and executive branches, has to determine the structure and the number of judges in each court. The Islamic State Supreme Court is solely responsible for appointing judges to all sorts of courts. The following structure of the judicial system is suggested as appropriate to the needs of today's Islamic Nation:

1. *The Supreme Court* is at the apex of the judicial structure. The Islamic State Supreme Court and, in turn, the Supreme Court of each province in the Islamic State, has final jurisdiction to decide all cases which may be brought before it by appeal or otherwise from the lower courts. Also, it has the final word over executive and legislative acts and statutes. Through its appellate jurisdiction, the Supreme Court maintains uniformity in the application of the law throughout the State. The Islamic State Supreme Court only has the final decision in the interpretation of the Islamic Holy Constitution.

2. *The Cassation Court* is next to the Supreme Court in the hierarchy. It reviews cases which involve capital crimes such as murder, theft, adultery and life imprisonment. It has final jurisdiction to decide all such cases without exception. The formality of procedures and records are complete in this type of court. Each province in the Islamic State shall have only one Court of Cassation.

3. *The Criminal Court* is the third level in the heirarchical order of the Islamic judicial system. Courts at this level are courts of record; that is, they keep complete and accurate statements of testimony and proceedings which may be reviewed by the higher courts if a case is appealed. The Criminal Court is specialized in all types of crimes requiring major penalties (i.e., death or life imprisonment), conducted against the State.

4. *The General Civil Court* is on the same level as the Criminal Court, but specializes in cases which do not require major punishment. It can also resolve commercial disputes.

5. *The Personal Statute Court* is on the same level as the General Civil Court. It specializes in problems of marriage, divorce, inheritance, and endowment and so forth.

6. *The Court of Summary* is at the base of the judiciary structure. The Summary Court's function is to pass sentence upon persons accused of misdemeanors and to decide petty civil disputes. In large cities, there may be specialized divisions of such courts. At this level, procedure is informal and records are often incomplete.

Personnel and Tenure of the Judiciary

Judicial work requires a thorough knowledge of the Islamic Holy Constitution, constitutional law (Sharīʾah), and the Islamic language; it also demands a thorough knowledge of contemporary social and economic conditions. At the personal level, it requires a developed judgement—the ability to be impartial and have non-partisan integrity. Judges must be guaranteed unconditional tenure and remuneration, to assure their independence from political influence. Accordingly judges may not work for more than twenty-five years. After their retirement, they must have their full salaries so they may be recruited for certain temporary missions by the Supreme Court or the administration. Moreover, judges may not work in the same court more than three consecutive years, with the exception of those who were chosen to be on the Supreme Court. Members' terms in the Cassation Courts may be extended to five years. The periodic movement of judges creates more intention to restrict application of the law and, in turn, of justice.

Bases for Selecting Judges

Because a judge requires extraordinary qualities and exceptional faculties, the selection of judges in the Islamic State is based on the following conditions, in addition to what has been mentioned in the election of the House of Jurists.

1. Outstanding knowledge of the Islamic language.
2. Distinct ability to understand the Islamic Holy Constitution regulations and their divergent applications.
3. Mastering the element of logic, especially the parts concerning analogy (qiyās).
4. Outstanding knowledge in extracting, extrapolating and formulating laws from the Islamic Holy Constitution.
5. Being completely sane and sound in body, decent, and with strength and fairness in the application of Islam in his own life (*see* Al-Māwardī, 1971, especially Vol. 1, pp. 618–44).

Members of the Supreme Court

The Islamic state Supreme Court may consist of seventeen members who may serve for a fixed term of eight years. They can be re-elected for only three terms. The Islamic Congress may nominate at least thirty jurists, either from the members of the House of the Jurists or from the outside. Candidates for membership in the Islamic State Supreme Court have to be elected by the Islamic Nation, following the same procedure as that of the members of the Congress. The seventeen jurists who gain the greatest majority in the vote will become members of the Supreme Court.

The provincial Supreme Court will be similar in function and election as the state Supreme Court. However, there will be only seven judges serving terms of six years. They may be re-elected for four terms.

THE EXECUTIVE

In a broad sense the executive branch is the dynamic branch of governmental order and power, representing and effecting the will of the Islamic State. Its discretionary power is great, for all the complex and multiform details of administration could not possibly be embodied in statutes. Although its major function is to execute the Islamic Holy Constitution and the Constitutional Law, the executive branch usually acts on many matters not covered by law. In a very real sense the executive branch is the nucleus of authority and the active force in the government. This is acknowledged by Muslims when they speak of the Caliphate of the Right-guided Caliphs, which carries similar connotations as the American 'administration' or the British 'government'.

The executive branch is responsible for much of the planning of the Islamic State. On the basis of its special knowledge and experience, the executive may suggest projects or techniques to the legislature. However, any abuse of power may lead the legislature to impose restrictions to prevent future performances of the same kind. Both the legislature and judiciary are essential checks on executive actions. The basis of this system derives from when the Prophet and his companions made what Muslim jurists called the performance of undesirable legislative acts in the Battle of Badr. The correction of law was immediately revealed by God to set right what had been done and restricted the Prophet to certain laws which prevented further future performance of the same act (*The Qur'ān* 8:167; 9:43).

Executive Powers and Functions

The powers and functions of the executive branch outlined below are the result of a careful study of the role of the Prophet and his four Right-guided successors (*see* Al-Ṭabarī, 1962; Ibn Hishām, 1955; Al-Kattānī, n.d.). In the Islamic system all executive powers, subject to a few limitations, are vested in a single chief executive. The President of the Islamic state, or the Caliph of the Islamic Nation, is personally responsible for enforcing all laws and court decisions. He has the right, in some instances, to insist upon a rigorous enforcement of the letter of the law, especially in forbidding things; otherwise he may seek to accomplish equivalent results by enforcing only the spirit (Muslim, *Faḍāʾil*, 130). The power to enforce the laws includes other powers appropriate to the chief executive. Essentially, he has the authority to appoint subordinates, to direct them in their duties and to remove subordinates who refuse or neglect to perform their duties.

The President of the Islamic State is personally responsible for formulating and executing administrative policy. Legislatures have come to rely upon the executive branch for working out the programmes to be accomplished, the methods to be used and the necessary organizational details. The legislature, when making statutes on relatively new subjects, cannot possibly forsee the complications and technicalities which may arise. Consequently, they establish only the main policy outlines and grant to the executive branch, with suitable safeguards, sub-legislative power. Through this power the executive issues ordinances that have the force of the law when they fill in the details necessary for the application of statutes to specific conditions. This may help explain why the Islamic Holy Constitution does not give a lot of detail at the times of revelation concerning matters that are liable to change and develop, especially those concerning the unseen future. Such complete details given for the existing situation, and therefore applicable only to a certain era and people, would confuse later believers by mentioning names and details not familiar to them.

The chief executive is the Commander-in-Chief of the armed forces of the Islamic State. He has the power to determine the movement and use of the military in times of peace and war. In wartime there is a tremendous concentration of power in the executive branch. Usually, in the event of war the legislature confers its power on the chief executive so that he may take all possible steps to resolve the conflict. The chief executive takes control of production and transportation, establishes rationing, institutes censorship and suspends certain guarantees of civil liberty. However, even when these powers are not so conferred, the executive branch may take any necessary actions to safeguard the state and ensure the successful prosecution of war.

The chief executive of the Islamic State is personally responsible for the formulation and execution of foreign policy. At his discretion, he may grant or withhold recognition of the government of a foreign state. He appoints, instructs and controls the activities of ambassadors, ministers and consuls, and directs other foreign service affairs. He may dismiss the ambassador or any foreign personnel of a foreign state. The chief executive decides what claims to territory, property and other rights to advance on behalf of his state or its citizens and permanent residents. He may send representatives to international assemblies and conferences to co-operate in the solution of world problems. He has exclusive control of negotiation of treaties; major treaties, however, have to be validated by the Islamic Congress.

The executive branch has the power to issue pardons for offenses against the state either before or after trial and conviction, except in cases for which the penalties are prescribed by the Islamic Holy Constitution. The pardon either releases a person from the legal consequences of a crime or remits the penalty imposed. The chief executive may reduce a sentence or, by a reprieve, delay its execution, but he may not increase it. Also, he may issue a proclamation of amnesty, whereby a specifically described group of people is absolved from the legal consequences of rebellion or other action against the state.

Election and Tenure of the President

The chief executive shall be elected directly by the Muslim people. The Islamic Congress will nominate two or more persons from each division of the Islamic Congress, the House of the Jurists and the House of the Professionals. After the nomination, the Islamic Congress will meet and vote for two candidates only. The Chief Justice will put the two candidates on a ballot so that the Islamic Nation may choose one of them as the President of the Islamic State. If there is a Qurayshite candidate, the Islamic State Supreme Court has to declare his legal genealogical line in a special broadcast to the nation (*see* Muslim, *Īmārah*, 1–9). However, the president of the Islamic State must have fully memorized the Holy Qur'ān, have a very good knowledge of the Prophet's Sunnah and of Islamic history. The presidential term should be determined and fixed ten years and limited to one term only. This fixed term has been determined according to the approximate period of the Prophet of Islam who headed the first Islamic Nation in Medina. Long, fixed terms of office enable the executive to acquire experience and insure his independence and are conducive to consistent foreign and domestic policies. Ten years also gives the head of the state a free hand to pursue consistent policies without being affected by the fear of not being re-elected after serving one short term.

However, in case of the illness or death of the President of the Islamic State, the Vice President will take over until the Chief Justice officially declares the presidential office vacant. The Chief Justice will then request the Islamic Congress to nominate two candidates for public election. The Vice President may complete the term, if five or fewer years are left for the current administration.

In case of impeachment, high crime, misdemeanor or an obvious violation of the provision of the Islamic Holy Constitution, the Chief Justice shall ask the Islamic Congress to meet in irregular session. The Chief Justice, then, reads the decision of the Islamic State Supreme Court, which will indicate that the President of the Islamic State is no longer suitable for the office because of his violations and the Court's decision. In the same meeting, the Vice President will take the oath of office and take over as acting president until a new president can be elected, no later than one week after this incident unless the remaining time is five years or less. The Vice President may become one of the candidates for the presidential office in the general election.

The presidential election shall always be conducted at the tenth month of the Islamic calendar year. After his election, the new president will overlap the current president for two months attending meetings as an observer. On the first day of the new year (i.e., the first day of the month of Al-Muharram, he will be inaugurated in an official ceremony in a special session of the Islamic Congress. He will take the oath of office before the Chief Justice and the members of the state Supreme Court.

The Cabinet and Presidential Control

Once the elected candidate of the Islamic Congress for the presidential office receives the majority, he obtains all electoral votes accordingly. After his take-over, the new President of the Islamic State shall, within his first week, appoint his own advisors and cabinet officers. Officers shall be appointed within the Islamic Congress. The President has the right to choose up to four people for his cabinet out of the Islamic Congress, but they must be approved by the Islamic Congress and swear an oath of office before the Islamic State Supreme Court. The President of the Islamic State may invite, for a discussion of certain problems, people outside his 'official family' (all officers, including members of Congress, provincial governors and military staff); these discussions are informal, but secret. The cabinet may discuss matters affecting a single department or all departments and advise the President on any subject which he submits to them. The President may accept or ignore their advice or votes.

Presidential Power over Legislation

The Islamic Holy Constitution provides the President of the Islamic state with the following major legislative powers.

1. Originally the Islamic Holy Constitution required that a Presidential Declaration should be patterned after the Declaration of Medina. The President must assure the continuity of the application and implementation of the Islamic Holy Constitution, and also provide more security and better living for the Islamic Nation. He may articulate the government's major policy. A declaration enables the President to formulate and present to Congress and to the Islamic Nation as a whole a complete legislative program at the beginning of each session. The President, on the first Friday of his presidency, may lead the Friday prayer in the general mosque of the capital. After the prayer, he shall deliver the Presidential Declaration. An annual budget and economic address is also expected from the President to determine the State's responsibility towards national financial situations—especially in regard to those who partially or completely depend on State support. The budget and economic address shall be after the State has collected all types of income tax required by law.

2. The chief executive may issue a suspensive veto over legislation that is not basically derived from the Islamic Holy Constitution. His veto may be overriden by an adverse veto of at least two-thirds of the Islamic Congress. In this case, the Islamic State Supreme Court will determine the most suitable decision in keeping with the provisions of the Islamic Holy Constitution and the welfare of the Islamic Nation. The Court may support either opinion or make up new legislation. The Court's decision is final. The chief executive may also suspend any legislation of the Islamic Holy Constitution under severe and abnormal circumstances but not including Divine Services or personal statute.

3. The chief executive may influence the development of legislative programmes through the report and/or proposal of his cabinet members to Congress and, perhaps, by intimating to Congressional leaders that a proposed bill is satisfactory or unsatisfactory, with the result that a bill is approved, dropped or modified to suit his views.

4. The chief executive may call the attention of the people to the need for new legislation or for change in the existing laws. Such a presidential action may compel the Islamic Congress to act on measures that it had previously disapproved or delayed. He also possesses the power to issue executive decrees and proclamations under powers

granted to him by the Islamic Holy Constitution. He may call Congress and the Supreme Court into special session to consider his intention to declare war. In emergencies, the chief executive has to take full responsibility along with the Chief Justice and the head of the Islamic Congress.

The Office of Provincial Governor

Generally speaking, the office of governor of a province in the Islamic state conforms to the pattern of the presidential system except in the following:

1. The Islamic Congress nominates two people for each province, one from the House of Jurists and the other from the House of the Professionals, for public election in each province.

2. Nominees for each province must neither have been brought up in nor live in that province.

3. The governor in each province is solely responsible before the President of the Islamic state for the application of the Islamic Holy Constitution. The President can summon the governor for trial in the Islamic state Supreme Court for unconstitutional acts and/or decisions, but he cannot be removed from office unless the court finds him guilty.

4. In name, the governor is the chief executive in the province, but his constitutional power to control the administration is limited. Provincial officers, whether elected or appointed, are responsible to the law and are not subject to removal at the discretion of the Governor.

5. Tenure of the governor shall be fixed at four years and limited to two terms only in one province. All other administrative officers, with the exception of provincial congress members, shall be limited to six years and three terms only.

6. Generally, the governor's legislative powers are superior because he may veto separate items in appropriation bills. However, to exercise effective control over his administration, he must often request the legislature to make changes in those laws which are not derived from the Islamic Holy Constitution, according to the prevailing situation and need of the province.

In summary, the Islamic State's purposes and functions are not different from those of any other state. Moreover, Islam has emphasized the great responsibility of the state to provide three essential factors for the Islamic Nation: the complete security of the life and property of individuals within the state; the full responsibility of the Islamic State to provide a living for those who cannot work or do not find a decent job; and finally, the Islamic State has to spread and practise justice and equality among its subjects and all over the world.

In terms of governmental organization, Islam, for the first time in human history, has introduced the 'popular' factor in the selection of those in authority and those who run the affairs of state. As a consequence of this right, Islam has set up certain duties that have to be carried out by the Islamic Nation—they have to commit themselves and obey the authority they choose.

In addition to the spiritual role of the Prophet, his period in Medina as the head of that first Islamic State provides a great model for conducting the affairs of the state. The essential authority of the head of the state, such as Commander-in-Chief, has been practised by the Prophet during his ruling period in Medina.

Finally, development and change in the structure of the Islamic state governmental organization is necessary because the Islamic Holy Constitution does not precisely set up a fixed structure.

4

The Concepts of Peace and War in Islam

In Islam, the concepts of peace and war are, in general, based on one absolute fact: the Islamic Holy Constitution does not instruct by any means the Islamic Nation to wage perpetual war with those nations of the world not included under the sovereignty and jurisdiction of the Islamic State. Nor does it order Muslims to fight and kill all non-Muslim people throughout the world. Such an instruction would be unacceptable in any rational or logical way. The following Sunnah verse reminds Muslims that not all people can be Muslims:

> Certainly, God has contracted the earth to me until I have seen its Western and Eastern parts. Certainly my nation's supremacy will be to what has been contracted to me.
>
> Muslim, *Fitan*, 19

The Islamic Nation explicitly has not been ordered to fight the whole wold, as assured by the following verse:

> If God had willed, He would have rendered them [mankind] one nation but He admits whosoever He will into His mercy, and the iniquitous have neither protector nor patron.
>
> *The Qur'ān* 42:8

However, the concept of war in Islam may be construed as a phenomenon manifested in the nature of man. Whenever man discovers his strength and potency he often fails to restrain himself or to use his power in peaceful ways. War then becomes indispensable to him and, in order to satisfy his desires, he tries to master other men and to manipulate them to fulfill his whimsical dreams. Competition and visions of glory are behind every war. In this chapter we will discuss Islam's system of peace, Jihad and the rules of war in Islam.

Islam: The System of Peace

The Islamic system did not build its state, society and civilization on paralytic notions, searching for the ephemeral things of this world, but from the beginning has presented its appeal to mankind in a polite and peaceful way. The Prophet of Islam and his followers, for a period of some fifteen years, tried to convey peacefully the message of Islam. People at the time realized that Islam is a complete system, concerned above all with liberating people from idolizing other people (Al-Ṭabarī, 1962, Vol. 2, pp. 293–393).

Islam's basic mission is to spread justice and equality among all peoples, so every being can freely decide his or her own destiny. Subsequently the disbeliever relatives of the first believers started to oppress, outrage and threaten the Muslims unjustly. They even went so far as to incite and rally people around them to reject Islam and to exercise their ultimate aggression against Muslims (Al-Ṭabarī, 1962, Vol. 2, pp. 345–8). The Islamic Holy Constitution recognized that a forceful Muslim response to the aggressors during the infancy of the Islamic Nation would mean the complete destruction of the believers themselves, their families and their property. However, as time passed, the non-Muslims' aggressive acts increased so that the Messenger and the believers began to ask when and how God would be willing to help them. The answers were then revealed in two Qur'ānic verses which asserted that the help of God is assuredly near and His will is to let the believers experience aggression in order to test their sincerity and devotion to His message. The Test would not last forever (*The Qur'ān*, 2:214; 3:179).

Twice the believers were ordered by God to flee to Abyssinia after their patience had come to an end. However, even when they did manage to flee, the aggressors followed them to incite the Abyssinians against them (Al-Ṭabarī, 1962, Vol. 2, p. 335). For the thirteen following years, the believers were the target of an unpredictable assault and offensive by non-Muslims. Finally the order came to the Prophet, telling him and his followers to flee to Medina, the first Islamic territory. In Medina, the *Anṣār*, the Helpers, who embraced Islam, were bravely willing to provide a secure shelter for the followers of the new faith. On his arrival at Medina, the Prophet finally found the most significant factors necessary to declare the existence of the first Islamic State—the land and the population. Immediately he issued the first Islamic declaration of independence in the world, known as 'The Declaration of Medina'. Almost all the emigrants who fled to Medina left their homes and wealth in Makkah, all of which was confiscated by the non-Muslims. This specific event is documented in the Islamic Holy Constitution in the following Qur'ānic verse:

> [Fay', booty from the surrendered army is] for the poor immigrants who have been expelled out of their habitations and their wealth, for the sake, bounty and blessing of God, patronizing for God and His Prophet, those are certainly the truthful.
>
> *The Qur'ān*, 59:8

Not until almost two years after the prophet established the Islamic State in Medina was the order to counter the aggression revealed. It is the first Qur'anic verse dealing with the concept of warfare in Islam:

> Permission is given to those who are attacked [to counterattack] because they have been tyrannized; God, indeed is able to bestow victory upon them. Those who were expelled out of their habitations unlawfully only because they say our sovereign is God. Had not God driven back some of the people by means of others there would be destruction of monasteries, churches, synagogues, and mosques in which the name of God is much commemorated. God promises to bestow victory upon those who exert themselves for Him. God assuredly is Powerful and Supreme.
>
> *The Qur'ān*, 22:39–40

These two verses delineate one of the basic dimensions of warfare in Islam: whenever Muslims are tyrannized and/or expelled from their homes only because they are Muslims, they have to attack the aggressors. Another aspect can also be extracted from the second verse. War is considered in Islam as a phenomenon manifested in the nature of man. This manifestation is usually exercised by powerful men to defend their positions, compete with others for material interests, and glorify themselves by enslaving others. It is, then, God who gives victory to those who are lawfully fighting to protect the Word of God. Another verse of the Holy Qur'ān dealing with the same topic emphasizes and considers aggression as corruption in the earth: 'Had not God driven back some of the people by means of others the earth would be corrupted' (2:251). Thus unlawful war is generally considered by the Islamic Holy Constitution as a corruption in the earth. So, can war be waged by the Islamic State in terms of law rather than in terms of what has been mentioned above? Actually, in two more lawful situations the Islamic State can wage war: in a condition of general defence of the state and in the condition of participating in the liberation of other societies who have been exposed to aggression.

In summary and, after this brief account of the condition of Muslims at the very inception of the Islamic message, the conclusion is that Islam basically is not, by any means, an aggressive system. Considering the period in which Islam did not order its first followers even to counterattack the grievous aggression they faced, the instruction of Islam has always called for peace, brotherhood and human consideration. Islam, in fact, is the first system in human history that firmly determines and confines the purposes of war to defence and to release from grievous aggression. It carefully delineates the most significant rules of human rights during war. Finally, Islam never instructs its followers to wage war for glory or competition for any sort of materialistic interest.

Jihād

The root of the term Jihād is the verb *jahada*, which means 'to exert', used in the Islamic Holy Constitution in the same meaning as in common Arabic usage and in the lexical meaning (see Ibn Manzur, n.d., v.s., Jahada). However, the Islamic Holy Constitution has restricted the exertion of Muslims themselves to the cause or path of God in three major areas: to defend the Islamic Nation from any outside attack; to liberate people from any aggressive power; and to call people to Islam and convey its message to all people in terms of courtesy and consideration. Of course, the exertion of the Muslims themselves is required in all kinds of acts in their lives and should be done perfectly and sincerely, especially during Divine Services. However, Jihād is always emphasized in these three aspects by the Islamic Holy Constitution.

To accomplish such targets well, especially the defence of the Islamic State, Islam has constituted, for the first time in human history, the law of conscription. Certainly such a law was not known to the world before the Islamic message was revealed. It is the Islamic Holy Constitution which established such a law first.

> Warfare, has been written [ordained] upon you although it's hateful to you, verily you may hate a thing which is best for you and you may love a thing which is harmful for you. God knows and you do not know.
>
> *The Qur'ān*, 2:216

Accordingly, learning to fight is an obligatory task ordained by God to every individual Muslim, except the handicapped and the blind who are excluded completely from learning to fight and from participating on the battle field.

> Surely, they are not equal, those believers who do not respond to the call to arms, with the exception of those who are disabled, and those who exert themselves in the cause of God personally and with their wealth.
>
> *The Qur'ān*, 4:95

The handicapped in general are dismissed from conscription and in turn from participating in fighting. The verse also refers to the great inequality between those who participate and those who prefer to stay behind.

The second group, exempted from participating in battle but not from learning to fight, are those Muslims who devote themselves to the study of the Islamic Holy Constitution. By learning to fight, they are considered a reserve force for any emergency call.

> It is not the standard for the believers to respond collectively to the call to arms. But, it should have been a group from each unit devoting themselves to the study and comprehension of the legal knowledge of Islam. So, they will be a reference for their people when they return to them that they may be aware.
>
> *The Qur'ān*, 9:122

Two rules can be extracted from this verse. The first is the necessity for having a reserve force for any emergency other than those who have been assigned for the security of the State, called the *muriābiṭūn* or the National Guard. For practical purposes, the reserve forces have to devote themselves to the study of the Islamic Holy Constitution, to become religious teachers for their brothers when they return. It is also a great advantage for those teachers to know about the practical uses of weapons used on the battlefield. The second rule is that God rewards equally both the fighters and the reserve forces who study the legal knowledge of Islam, a concept derived from the verse's use of the term *nafara*, to respond, for both the fighters and the students. The deliberate use of the same verb indicates that God's reward is the same for both groups. It also indicates that gaining legal knowledge of Islam is obligatory.

JIHĀD: DEFENCE OF THE ISLAMIC NATION

The Islamic Holy Constitution orders the Islamic Nation to prepare its ultimate power to defend the Islamic State's territorial jurisdiction and boundaries from any unexpected attack by an external, belligerant power. Such an order is asserted in the three Qur'ānic verses below which establish the concept of defensive war in Islam.

> Make [plural imperative] ready for them [the non-Muslims] and muster all your powers as you can, and station the national guard at your boundary to intimidate thereby the enemies of God and your enemies and others behind them whom you do not know but whom God knows. So, whatever you sacrifice in the cause of God, you will be completely rewarded for, and you will never be treated unjustly.
>
> *The Qur'ān*, 8:60

> And fight in the cause of God those who attack you, but do not be aggressive; verily God does not love the aggressors.
>
> *The Qur'ān*, 2:190

> And they will continuously attack you in order to turn you back from Islam if they can.
>
> *The Qur'ān*, 2:217

These three verses provide logical instructions for the concept of defensive war in Islam. The first emphasizes the necessity for the Islamic State to prepare its power and the importance to preserve the State's will and its potential sovereignty. The second verse determines clearly the basic principle of defensive war. It orders the Islamic Nation not to instigate aggression or declare war unless it is attacked, when counterattack is certainly required. It also opens the door for Muslims to contribute voluntarily to the defence of their State; such a contribution is considered equal to jihād in terms of God's reward. The last verse completes the service in predicting and warning Muslims that non-Muslims never have and never will give up their attempt to demolish Islam, not only by fighting but by all possible means. Their ultimate goal is to drive Muslims away from their belief. It is obvious that their main purpose is to substitute God's sovereignty over Muslims with that of their own, which would allow them to dominate and direct Muslims according to their own will.

However, if the impossible had become a reality and the non-Muslims gave up their aggressive attempts, then Muslims should be prepared for such an eventuality and carry out the order of the Islamic Holy Constitution.

> God does not forbid you to be faithful and to deal justly with those who do not attack you and do not drive you from your land because you are Muslim. God certainly loves those who are just.
>
> *The Qur'ān*, 60:8

Finally, these defensive instructions are emphasized in a verse from the Sunnah, which underscores the necessity of having a stationed army around the Islamic Nation, the *ribaṭ*.

> Defence of one day [for defending the Islamic Nation's boundary] in the cause of God [its reward] is better than to have possession of the whole world and whatever it contains.
>
> Muslim, *Īmārah*, 163; Al-Bukhārī, *Jihād*, 73

The second verse of the above group of three uses the term 'enemy', *'aduw*, to refer to the non-Muslims. It is impossible here to accept the interpretation of common Arabic usage, or any other usage, of the term in question in which the enemy means to harbour strong feelings of hatred. Certainly such malicious feelings cannot be held by God Himself, nor should they be harboured by Muslims against God's creation. If Muslims harboured malice, then it would be very difficult to welcome non-Muslims into brotherhood when they adopt Islam.

On the other hand, the Islamic Holy Constitution has proclaimed that even God will be delighted when his servant repents and returns to His right path (Muslim, *Tawbah*, 1–8). Thus, the term 'enemy' must be used in the same way as in the original Arabic lexicon which refers to the general divergence in opinion or belief (Ibn Manẓūr, n.d., s.v. *ʿadā*). Consequently, this general differentiation can be restricted to the divergence of Muslims and non-Muslims in believing the Islamic message. Considering this meaning of the term 'enemy', the Islamic Holy Constitution continuously prohibits Muslims from patronizing non-Muslims (the Holy Qurʾān 3:28; 4:51). Such prohibitions indicate that Muslims must not hold malevolent feelings towards non-Muslims and also must not consider the non-Muslims clients or patrons.

Finally, destructive hostility, which is generally based on material interests, race, colour and sex, must not diminish the feelings of Muslims for any human being. The Islamic Holy Constitution does not give Muslims the right to claim superiority over non-Muslims. Superiority in Islam can be achieved by any individual who devotes himself to God by means of purety, piety and righteous deeds as declared in the following verse of the Holy Qurʾān:

> O, mankind, verily We have created you from a single male and female, and rendered you nations and tribes for knowing. Surely the most superior of you in the sight of God is the most pious one, thereupon God is Omniscient and Expert.
>
> *The Qurʾān*, 49:13

JIHĀD: SALVATION AND LIBERATION FROM INIQUITY

The idea of a human god, who dictates his will and enforces specific human doctrines over nations and societies has continuously coloured human history, no matter what the nation's role in prompting human civilization. Although there have been basic changes in names and techniques, kings, emperors, tyrants and finally imperialism and socialism have set up as their major goals one person or idea to be recognized as the absolute power. In effect, the main intention is to facilitate the manipulation of mankind towards the goals of the elite who in turn become intoxicated by the use of power.

However, human beings by their limited power cannot easily discover the existence of God as the Sole Sovereign. God's justice dictates that He will never punish any of his noblest creatures unless they know about Him and His sovereign power through His messengers. In fact, the major goal behind God's revelations and messengers are to introduce God to His creatures so that they may recognize and worship Him alone. The Islamic Holy Constitution has insured, as a promise from God Himself, that He will never punish anyone who had not heard about Him.

> Read your book [in Resurrection Day everybody will be given his own record in which he will find all he has done and he will be told] it is enough for you to be your own reckoner on this day. Whosoever accepts right-guidance does so only for himself, and whosoever goes astray does only for himself and nobody bears the load of another. We [God] never punish anyone until We have certainly sent a messenger.
>
> *The Qur'ān* 17:14–15

In addition to conveying God's message, His messengers have been appointed by God to be witnesses on the Day of Resurrection over their nation. The Islamic Holy Constitution asserts this doctrine:

> And on the Day [the Resurrection] We will raise up from every nation a witness, then, there will be no leave for those who disbelieve, nor will they be blamed.
>
> *The Qur'an* 16:84

Accordingly, the messengers' missions are not completed until they have testified before God that they conveyed the messages with which they were sent. Consequently there will be no excuse given to those who rejected the light of God and choose their own direction.

At first sight, these two doctrines imply that God will not punish any human being unless He first sends a messenger and the messenger will be a witness against his people. These doctrines may contravene another famous doctrine in Islam which proclaims that the messages of God are sealed by the Prophet Muḥammad who is the final messenger of God. The Islamic Holy Constitution emphasizes this doctrine in many verses of the Holy Qur'ān and Sunnah as indicated in the following verses.

> Muḥammad has not been and never will be a father of any man of you, but he is certainly the Messenger of God and the Seal of the Prophets, and God is Omniscient.
>
> *The Qurʾān* 33:40

> The Prophet has said: I am the seal of the Prophets.
>
> Muslim, *Faḍāʾil*, 22

To eliminate any apparent discrepancy between this doctrine and the two others above, Islam has established two more doctrines that clarify the matter. The first has proclaimed Islam a universal system of life, polity, society and religion for all mankind and to the end of time, from the time of the Prophet forever. This doctrine has been delineated by many verses of the Islamic Holy Constitution, including the ones above and those below:

> And we have surely sent you to all beings, entirely, as precursor [to indicate the approach of the hour] and, as consecrator [to cannonize the reward and punishment of those who accept or reject the message of God, respectively] but most of mankind does not know [the difference between right and wrong].
>
> *The Qurʾān* 34:28

> And we have certainly sent you as a mercy for all beings.
>
> *The Qurʾān* 21:107

The universality of the message of Islam is explicit in these verses. The second verse, however, portrays Islam as a liberation and a system of salvation for all beings regardless of their faith, creeds or laws. In the second doctrine, the Islamic Holy Constitution has ordered and appointed the Nation of Islam, individually as well as collectively to bear witness to mankind by conveying the Islamic message to them.

> Thus We have rendered you a *midmost nation* for the purpose of being witnesses over mankind as the Prophet is being a witness over you.
>
> *The Qurʾān* 2:143

> And exert yourself in the cause of God with all conceivable effort, He has appointed you and will never deceive you by the means of

religion [Islam]—the tenet of your Father Abraham. He [God] named you Muslim in this message as He named His worshipers long ago [The purpose of this appointment is that] as the Prophet will be a witness over you, you will be witnesses over mankind, so perform prayers, pay *zakāh* (the income tax) and hold on to God. He is your Sovereign, He is, indeed, the Protector and the Patron.

The Qurʾān 22:78

It is your mission to convey even one verse of mine to the people.

Al-Bukhārī, *Anbiyāʾ*, 50

According to these verses, the Islamic Nation has been commissioned by God to convey the message of Islam to all beings continuously, without exception. Considering the responsibility of conveying Islam to non-Muslims, all Muslims will hold this testimonial position before God on the Day of Resurrection against any being who denies knowing the message of Islam. On the other hand, all Muslims will be held accountable for not propagating Islam throughout the world and to all beings. Where the message is easily propagated there absolutely is no need to fight. But Muslims must fight the powerful, so-called, human gods and crumble their aggressive power when such self styled gods try to prevent their people from knowing any doctrine except that dictated to them. Such powers even exceed the role of God whose messengers were never allowed to indoctrinate people by means of force. The Islamic Holy Constitution, to eliminate such so-called gods from power and liberate the people so they may freely choose the creeds they want, has commanded the Islamic Nation vigorously to fight such powers. It orders Muslims not to stand helpless while other people are being indoctrinated and treated unjustly and aggressively. The command has come in many Qurʾānic verses, including the following:

The track [to fight and/or oppress] is open only against those who tyrannize mankind and unlawfully commit outrages in the earth, those shall have painful chastisement.

The Qurʾān 42:42

And attack them until there is no dissention, oppression or compulsion, and until the people have the freedom of choice in total sub-

> mission to God. Thereupon, if they quit, God certainly is aware of what they are doing.
>
> *The Qur'ān* 8:39

Thus, fighting for reasons other than defence is also required of the Islamic Nation so they may carry out and fulfill the will of God, i.e., to demolish human gods on the earth, to propagate justice and equality and to let people decide freely their own destiny. This is, in fact, the main idea of jihād—to fight against such power only and never against mankind as a whole. The Islamic Holy Constitution reinforces this concept in the Sunnah verse, 'I, the Prophet, have been ordered to fight people until there is no god but God' (Muslim, *Iman*, 32). This order does not mean, however, that people should be fought until they become Muslims.

JIHĀD: THE CALL TO ISLAM

Explaining Islam to other people continuously until every human being knows about the existence of the Islamic message is, in fact, the basic idea of jihād. It is the only way to fulfill the command of God, Who appoints Muslims to stand witness over mankind. It is important to point out here that Muslims are restricted to conveying Islam, not to forcing their beliefs on others. They also should not expect any positive results of their mission because people are free to choose whatever faith they like.

> Call to the path of your God [that is to Islam] with wisdom and fair exhortation, and argue with them [the non-Muslims] in courtesy and considerate manner. Verily your God knows those who have gone astray and those who have been guided.
>
> *The Qur'ān* 16:125

> This is [Islam] an announcement for mankind to warn with.
>
> *The Qur'ān* 14:52

> Your mission is to convey [the message of God only].
>
> *The Qur'ān* 3:20

This is the role of a Muslim, to act as a 'witness' over mankind and to exert himself to warn and convey the message of God without expecting any result.

Finally, jihād offers three ways for Muslims to follow in the path of God: to abolish any iniquitous power which forces a certain ideology on its people, to call to Islam and convey the message of God to all people and to defend the Islamic Nation from any attack. It is obvious that Muslims have never had and never will have any intention of killing the non-Muslims throughout the world.

The Rules of War in Islam

The Islamic rules for wartime etiquette carry the force of law, because they are injunctions from God and His Prophet. These rules are strictly followed and applied by Muslims in all circumstances, irrespective of the behaviour of their enemy. They show that Islam fourteen centuries ago adopted standards of civilized and human warfare behaviour, which are far superior to any behaviour in today's civilized world.

1. Islam draws a clear and firm distinction between combatants and non-combatants in an enemy country. As far as the non-combatant population is concerned—women, children, the old, the infirm—the instructions of the Islamic Holy Constitution are written in verses of the Sunnah: 'Do not kill any old person, any child, or any woman' (Al Bukhārī, *Jihād*, 71), 'Do not kill the monks in the monasteries' (Al-Bukhārī, *Jihād*, 171; Ibn Ḥanbal, Vol. 3, p. 152) and 'Do not kill people who are sitting in the place of worship' (Al Bukhārī, *Jihād*, 171). During war the Prophet of Islam saw the corpse of a woman lying on the battleground and observed: 'She was not fighting, how then did she come to be killed' (Al-Bukhārī, *Jihād*, 19). From these statements of the Prophet's Sunnah, the conclusion can be drawn that those who are non-combatants must not be killed during or after war.

2. In regard to combatants, the Islamic Holy Constitution forbids torture by fire. The Prophet's Sunnah says 'Punishment by fire does not behove anyone except the Master of Fire' (Al-Bukhārī, Jihād, 19). The injunction deduced from this verse is that the adversary should not be burnt alive under any circumstances.

3. Wounded soldiers who are not fit to fight, nor actually fighting, must not be attacked and must be protected and hospitalized. The order to treat and care for wounded soldiers comes in the Sunnah verse, 'Do not attack a wounded person' (Al-Bukhārī, *Jihād*, 62).

4. Prisoners-of-war must not be killed, even though the enemy kills Muslim prisoners. As the Sunnah verse states, 'No prisoner should be

put to sword' (Ibn Ḥanbal, Vol. 4, p. 152). Other verses of the Sunnah prohibit killing any prisoner who is tied or is in captivity (Al-Bukhārī, *Jihād*, 17).

5. Muslims have been instructed by the Islamic Holy Constitution not to pillage, plunder or destroy residential areas, nor harm the property of anyone who is not fighting. The order comes in the Sunnah verse, 'Loot is no more lawful than carrion' (Al-Bukhārī, *Jihād*, 22). The first Right-guided Caliph, Abū Bakr, used to advise soldiers on their way to war, 'Do not destroy the villages and towns, do not spoil the cultivated fields and gardens, and do not slaughter the cattle' (Al-Bukhārī, *Jihād*, 22). Muslims have concluded that such prohibitions could not have been ordered by Abū Bakr unless he had heard them from the Prophet himself. They consider these orders as the provisions of the Islamic Holy Constitution. However, the rules governing the taking of booty from the battleground are altogether different. Booty consists of the wealth, provisions and equipment captured from the camps and military headquarters of the combatant armies and it may legitimately be appropriated.

6. A Muslim army does not have the right to use anything belonging to the people of a conquered country without paying for it or having the owners' consent and permission. The first Right-guided Caliph, Abū Bakr, used to instruct the Muslim army being dispatched to the battle front not even to use the milk of the cattle without permission of their owners (Al-Bukhārī, *Jihād* 85–6).

7. The Islamic Holy Constitution has categorically prohibited its followers from mutilating the corpses of their enemies, as was usually done by world nations before and after the advent of Islam. 'It is prohibited to mutilate the corpses of the enemy' (Ibn Hishām, 1955, Vol. 2, p. 134). The occasion on which this order was given is highly instructive. In the battle of Uḥud the enemy ripped open the stomach of Ḥamzah, the Prophet's uncle, and his liver was taken out and eaten by a woman from the enemy's camp. The Muslims were naturally enraged by this horrible sight, but the Prophet asked his followers not to mete out similar treatment to the dead bodies of the enemy. In the battle of Aḥzāb a renowned enemy warrior was killed and his body fell into a Muslim's trench. The non-Muslims presented ten thousand gold dinars to the Prophet and requested that the body of their fallen warrior be handed over to them. The Prophet replied, 'I do not sell dead bodies, you can take away the corpse of your fallen comrade' (Ibn Hishām, 1955, Vol. 2, p. 134).

8. The Islamic Holy Constitution has strictly prohibited treachery of any kind. Many examples in Qur'ānic verses and the Prophet's Sunnah affirm this provision, but the famous incident of Hudaybiyyah is the only one to be cited here. After the settlement of the terms of the treaty of Al-Hudaybiyyah, Abū Jandal, the son of the emissary of the non-Muslims who had negotiated the treaty with the Muslims, came bound and blood-stained to the Muslim's camp crying for help. The Prophet told him, 'Since the terms of the treaty have been settled, we are not in a position to help you. You should go back with your father. God will provide you with some other opportunity to escape this persecution' (Ibn Hishām, 1955, Vol. 2, p. 137). However, the entire Muslim army was deeply touched and grieved at the plight of Abū Jandal and many of them were moved to tears. But when the Prophet declared, 'We cannot break the agreement', not a single person came forward to help the unfortunate prisoner, so the non-Muslims forcibly dragged him back to Makkah.

These rules of war in Islam show that they are designed carefully to preserve humanity from undue suffering and torture. The rules have been held by Muslims as a part of their faith, and practised over the centuries from the inception of Islam. Whenever Muslims were involved in war, even though non-Muslims did not have similar restraints, or rules of warfare, the rules were followed. To disobey would have brought punishment by God. In summing up the concept of peace and war in Islam, one can conclude that Islam is not only the system of peace, but also the system that cares for all human beings, especially those who are unfortunate, who are exposed to ill-treatment and who are forced to practise specific creeds.

The idea of Jihād is continuously emphasized by the Islamic Holy Constitution, which indicates three different doctrines. Though the word Jihād itself does not indicate or refer to belligerency, it does mean that all individuals should strive in the path of God. The concept of enmity in Islam refers only to the difference in belief, and is not based on any antagonistic feeling directed by material interest, race, colour or sex. The three phases in which jihād can be directed are to defend the Islamic territories, to liberate people who are forced to beliefs against their will and to call to Islam and convey its message to all people. To achieve such goals, Islam has invented for the first time in human history the law of conscription. So every Muslim, with the exception of the disabled, has to learn to fight. Islam also differentiates between the reserve forces and those forces which have to be stationed around the state to secure its boundary. Finally, the Islamic Holy Constitution has enacted certain rules that have to be followed by Muslims during war. The first of these rules emphasizes that the Muslim army is not to kill women, children and older men who are not able to defend themselves. No other law in human history has had any such injunction to exclude such people from being killed. The Islamic order explicitly denotes the peaceful trend of Islam and its concern for human interactions. Also it indicates that killing for satisfaction, power or dominance had not been and never should have been practised by Muslims.

5

The Economy of the Islamic State: The Major Aspects

The economic system of Islam is designed to support the broad requirements of Muslims' lives, and to further justice and equality in Islamic society and between it and the world. It was realized at the outset of Islam that wealth is one of the greatest sources of power for man, a power which can effectively be used either constructively or destructively. Although it does not place any restriction on individual ownership or commercial freedom, Islam has positively adopted and formulated certain principles to regulate both activities. These regulations are aimed at determining man's potential for using negatively the power generated by personal wealth. Such destructive uses of power affect the ideal concepts of justice and equality and tend to serve power interests only (Dorfman, 1946, pp. 269–70, 416, 425–6; Demaris, 1974, Chapters 1, 2, 4 and 5). In general, the Islamic Holy Constitution has confirmed in many verses (*see*, for example, the *Holy Qur'ān* 21:55; 24:32; 26:88; 27:36) that man's ownership of wealth must be construed and conceived figuratively. This concept is emphasized because the real owner must be eternal: the real owner of everything is, thus, God alone Who is the only eternal one. Subsequently man's ownership must be interpreted as a temporary trust for the duration of his life. The Islamic Holy Constitution has, in fact, assured in the Prophet's Sunnah actual ownership by man. It states that 'man is the real owner of whatever he has consumed in his life; otherwise, whatever he has left of wealth actually belongs to those who possess such wealth after him' (Muslim, *Zuhd*, 3, 4). So man, in regard to whatever he possessed in his life, is only a trustee of such wealth and has to use it for his practical needs.

Because of the broad and detailed regulations of the economic system of Islam, in this chapter only two main topics will briefly be discussed: the major economic principle in Islam and the Islamic State national income.

Major Principles of the Islamic Economic System

The concentration of wealth, either by the state through its domination of national production or in the hands of a certain group of people, is the most significant phenomenon that the Islamic system has to counter and treat. The concentration of wealth is a difficult problem, because the unjust and unequitable result is the creation of a great gap within a society. Although the production of wealth is important and necessary, much more important is the way in which wealth is distributed within the nation. The concentration of wealth in the state, the main productive and commercial body of a nation's economy, adds another type of power to those who run the state's affairs. The concentration of wealth and power inevitably divides society into two major classes, the rulers and the ruled, those in power who enjoy their lives and those who toil for a living and always serve as labourers. In addition, the elite's domination of economic productivity and marketing may create a third class, the kings of wealth who may influence the politicians to act in their favour rather than that of the state. They may also participate personally in the state's affairs. Such a system always creates a huge class of labourers who can never be independent, cannot liberate themselves and have little hope of lifting themselves above the labouring level. Equal opportunity is thus only partially practised among classes, contradicting the democratic process. Consequently, the gap between rich and poor cannot be narrowed in such systems.

The Islamic system realizes that wealth must not be circulated among the rich people alone. This concept is confirmed by the Islamic Holy Constitution:

> Whatever booty from a surrendered army God has bestowed on His Prophet from the people of rural communities, it must be returned to God and His Prophet [that is the Islamic State, and to be distributed to] and the [poor] relatives of the Prophet, the orphans, the poor, and needy travellers, [this is ordained] lest such wealth become a source of increasing power for the rich amongst you.
>
> *The Qur'ān* 59:7

This verse states the major principle that governs the necessity of distributing wealth in the Islamic State. It indicates that justice does not mean the distribution of the income of the Islamic State to all sections of the Muslim Nation, nor its retention in the state treasury, but to equalize the distribution of wealth in the Islamic Nation.

Accordingly,the Islamic Holy Constitution has prescribed certain legal and optional measures to achieve a balance of wealth and to realize the objective of the welfare of the Islamic Nation by the equitable distribution of wealth. Of course, the main purpose of these regulations is to stop the concentration of wealth in a few hands. Thus, the greatest service Islam has done for humanity is that it has, once and for all, shattered the locked safes of the few and brought their accumulated wealth into circulation.

However, these legal provisions do not prohibit private ownership or restrict a free market. They are carefully designed to smooth the economy of Islam and to provide the original right for every individual to build up his own wealth without exploitation. In effect some of these provisions are naturally designed to increase individual ownership, materially and morally.

LEGAL MEASURES

In order to achieve the just and equitable distribution of wealth in the Islamic Nation and to decrease the concentration of wealth in a few hands, the Islamic Holy Constitution has prescribed the following provisions that consist of positive and prohibitive rules.

Positive Provision

Two main areas have been regulated by the Islamic Holy Constitution which effectively influences the diffusion of wealth annually and in each generation.

THE LAW OF INHERITANCE The Islamic Holy Constitution has laid down in three Qur'ānic verses (4:11, 12 and 176) the law of inheritance, which has to be followed exactly when dividing any legacy. Another Qur'ānic verse states that 'these are the statutes of God' (4:13). Thus the law of inheritance has to be applied in all cases, whether the legacy is small or large, an estate or money. Certainly the Islamic law of inheritance plays a significant role in lessening the inequality in the division of wealth in the Islamic Nation in each generation as it effectively reduces the everlasting gulf between the rich and poor. Therefore, the Islamic law of inheritance is a powerful and effective measure, both in checking accumulation of wealth and in diffusing it among large sections of the Islamic Nation. In regard to large estates, especially agrarian land, which cannot be divided or to do so would be harmful to its productivity, the Islamic State Supreme Court has to allocate the revenue among the inheritors in accordance with the law.

According to the Islamic law of inheritance, debts or any financial claim on the deceased's wealth have priority over all other claims. Before further distribution, the will of the deceased has to be considered (*The Holy Qur'ān* 4:12, 13). In this respect, the Islamic Holy Constitution allows a Muslim to allocate a maximum of one-third of his wealth to charity but never for any special inheritors. However, the Islamic Holy Constitution recommends giving an indefinite portion of the legacy to those who are present at the division and do not have a prescribed share, from among the relatives, orphans and poor (*The Holy Qur'ān* 4:8). Finally, the children of the deceased usually exclude all other relatives except the parents or grandparents. At the same time, the forebears' shares, and that of the wife or husband, are usually decreased by the shares of the children of the deceased.

In addition, the Islamic State is fully responsible for the deceased's debts and property when he leaves no inheritors or wealth. The following Sunnah verse of the Islamic Holy Constitution has determined this responsibility.

> I [the Prophet as the head of the Islamic State] am nearer to every Muslim than his ownself, so whoever leaves behind a debt or children to be supported, it shall be our charge; and whosoever leaves property, it is for his heirs; and I am the heir of the person who has no heirs—I inherit his property and liberate his captivity.
>
> Al-Bukhārī, *Farā'iḍ*, 4; Ibn Ḥanbal, 1969, Vol. 4, p. 133

Thus, the Islamic law of inheritance is designed to have far reaching effects. It does not allow wealth to accumulate in the hands of a few people, but helps to a certain degree to increase the circulation of wealth as well as its distribution among a large number of people. The Islamic law of inheritance, in effect, uproots the capitalist system in a few generations by distributing the wealth of the deceased among his near and distant relatives and poor neighbours. Above all, it provokes the Muslim to work and build up his own wealth rather than depending upon his inherited wealth, although he has a certain right to it.

ZAKĀH—THE SYSTEM OF TAXATION All Muslims, who own a minimum amount of unused property are liable for payment of zakāh and have been commanded by the Islamic Holy Constitution either to pay *zakāh* or an annual tax. Zakāh is the only annual tax Muslims have to pay in Islam, since it is a religious duty connected with faith and belief. It is considered the third pillar of the Islamic System. The Islamic Holy Constitution has laid great emphasis on its payment. In fact, whenever Muslims have been ordered to perform prayers by the Islamic Holy Constitution, they are also enjoined to pay zakāh (*The Holy Qur'ān* 2:3, 2:43, and 9:18). Zakāh is the second legal measure adopted by the Islamic System to prevent the concentration of wealth and to promote its diffusion among people. It is a compulsory levy tax that is collected by the Islamic State.

However, the main purpose of zakāh is threefold: to meet the needs of the poor and the destitute so that there are no needy people in the Islamic Nation; to lessen the accumulation of wealth in rich people's hands; and, finally, to purify and to increase the wealth of individuals as promised by God Himself. It is only collected from those who possess more wealth than they need. The Islamic State then distributes the collected zakāh to those who have less than their needs.

Prohibitive Measures

Different sorts of prohibitive legal measures are adopted by the Islamic System to attain its objective of social justice and equality within the Islamic Nation.

IḤTIKĀR—MONOPOLY Monopoly—the exclusive control of commodities of services in a particular market, especially the control and manipulation of prices—has been condemned by the Islamic Holy Constitution. The Arabic word *malʿūn*, meaning 'accursed of God', has been used in the Sunnah to describe the monopolizer, who is driven away from God's mercy forever unless, of course, he repents (Ibn Mājah, *Tijārah*, 6; Ibn Ḥanbal, Vol. 1, p. 21; Muslim, *Musāgāh*, 129, 130; *Muwaṭṭā'*, *Buyūʿ*, 56). The Islamic Holy Constitution emphasizes the prohibition of monopoly. Monopolies concentrate wealth in few hands and do not permit competition in a free market which is encouraged by the Islamic economic system. A Sunnah verse describes the free market as a market devoid of the monopolization of commodities and/or services. Monopolization of goods and services imposes restrictions on markets, consumers and small business. In fact, the main idea behind monopoly is to furnish wealth for a few people in society and to preserve to a large degree the gap between the poor and rich. It is for that reason that the Islamic Holy Constitution proscribes monopoly once and for all. Islam condemns the devilish idea of monopoly to assure a just and equitable social order represented by the competition of democracy.

RIBĀ — USURY Although ribā is proscribed because of its illegal interest, the Islamic Holy Constitution does not prohibit all kinds of interest. In fact, interest is proscribed only in the condition of ribā, which in Islam has two distinct meanings. The first may be defined as a loan given for personal use, such as to pay for a car or house. In this case a person who gets the loan pays either simple or compound interest out of his own pocket. Such a loan and its interest are designed to exploit the individual's money and effort with little risk to the capital, although individuals may benefit by owning the property. This kind of ribā tends to maintain a certain class of society in debt and under the manipulation of the rich community. For this reason, ribā is proscribed by the Islamic Holy Constitution in many Qur'ānic and Sunnah verses, two of which follow:

> Those who consume usury do not stand except as the one who is struck by the devil's touch; that is because they say: 'on the contrary, sale is just like usury'. God has legitimized sale, and has proscribed usury. So whosoever receives an admonition from his God and gives over, he shall have what has already passed, and his state has to be decided by God. And whosoever reverted—those are the Fire's inhabitants, therein dwelling forever.
>
> *The Qur'ān* 2:275

> O you who believe, fear God and relinquish what has remained [due] of usury if you are believers. But if you do not, then be warned of war [against you] from God and His Prophet. Yet if you repent, you shall have your principal [without interest] unwronging and unwronged.
>
> *The Qur'ān* 2:278–9

It is clear that these verses proscribe usury and refute the claim that usury is a state of sale.

The other phase of ribā which is also proscribed by the Islamic Holy Constitution is in the condition of exchange, either in money or commodities. Each kind of money or commodity has to be exchanged by the same amount if it is from the same kind; for instance, gold has to be exactly exchanged with gold in the same weight and measure. Any surplus of the same kind is ribā. Finally, ribā is prohibited also for encouraging the wealthy to find other ways to invest their money and serve their society.

IDDIKHĀR—HOARDING Hoarding is different from monopoly. It is an accumulation of articles, money or other valuables, preserved for future use. Those who hoard their accumulated wealth are the real enemies of the Muslim Nation. They, in effect, squeeze the veins of industry and check the progress and development of the Islamic Nation. Their wealth instead should produce more wealth for their benefit and for the benefit of the Muslim community as well.

In order to remedy the evils which result from hoarding wealth, it is proscribed in the Islamic Holy Constitution, which both condemns those who hoard their wealth and details the severe punishment waiting for them in the hereafter:

> And those who hoard up gold and silver and do not spend them in the cause of God, announce to them a painful chastisement. On the day, these [gold and silver] will be heated in the fire of hell and their foreheads, their flanks and their backs will be cauterized therewith. [They will be told] this is what you were hoarding for yourselves; now taste of what you used to hoard.
>
> *The Qur'ān* 9:34–35

A very painful punishment awaits those who hoard their wealth and do not use it for the prosperity and development of their society. The verses also indicate that such use of wealth is a sort of spending in the cause of God. They indicate, too, that payment of zakāh does not absolve those who hoard their wealth from other obligations which they owe to their society. It is a unique clue which connects abstention from participating in the state's economic productivity with the punishment of God.

WASTEFUL EXPENDITURE The Islamic Holy Constitution has prohibited all kinds of wasteful and unreasonable expenditure on superfluities which encourage rich people to indulge in luxuries. This unhealthy practice has been condemned by the Islamic Holy Constitution:

> And give your relative his due, the needy and the needy traveller, but never squander. Surely, the squanderers are the brothers of the devil, and the devil is ever ingrate to his God.
>
> *The Qurʾān* 17:26–7

Thus, all methods of spending which can be dubbed 'squandering' have been proscribed by the verses above, including cases which may cause moral or social injury, such as immoral business speculation or black market dealings. In this respect, the Islamic State has been ordered by the Islamic Holy Constitution to take under its control and management all the properties of those owners who have squandered their wealth unreasonably and against the instructions of the Islamic Holy Constitution:

> And do not give the squanderers your wealth which God has rendered you the responsibility to maintain; and allocate a portion for them to spend in their living and tell them honourable words.
>
> *The Qurʾān* 4:5

Squanderers' wealth, accordingly, belongs to the Islamic Nation as long as they spend their wealth wastefully. The Islamic State, thus, has to place such people under guardianship.

Optional Measures

The optional measures which the Islamic Holy Constitution has prescribed for preventing the accumulation of wealth, represent all charities that help the society, the economy and the defense of the Islamic Nation. The Islamic Holy Constitution considers giving to charity as a loan to God Himself, Who will certainly multiply the reward for it as He will:

> Who is he that will lend God a good loan [that is, spending for charity] assuredly, God will multiply it for him manifold? God takes hold and outspends and to Him you will be returned.
>
> *The Qurʾān* 2:245

Finally, in order to achieve its objectivity toward creating ultimate social justice and equality, the Islamic Holy Constitution has recommended that a certain amount of property is to be given to poor people as an expiation for many sorts of sins (*The Holy Qurʾān* 58:3–4). However, these expiations are usually options, running from high amounts of money to the performance of special services to God.

National Income of the Islamic State

National income is the keystone in determining the legal personality of a state. By its means and power a state can provide the required services to the nation and function properly in terms of liabilities and the application of the law. Because of the importance of income, the Islamic Holy Constitution has provided instructions for Muslims to confirm a constant major and some minor sources of the Islamic State National income.

NATURAL RESOURCES

The first and most important source of the Islamic State's national income are its national resources. Accordingly the Islamic Holy Constitution has confirmed in a Sunnah verse that 'people are partners in three: water, salt and pasture' (Al-Bukhārī, *Shurb*, 13; Ibn Mājah, *Ruhūn* 16; Ibn Ḥanbal, 1969 Vol. 5, p. 264). These are the most significant and necessary natural resources for sustaining human beings and animals. Through analogy—*qiyās*—all natural resources that can be discovered on land or in the sea must be shared by all peoples. The Islamic State is the only legal agency that has the right to own such national resources. Natural resources, thus, must be used in the welfare, defence and services of the Islamic Nation. The Islamic State, according to the text referenced above, may provide assistance to any part of the world which has suffered any national misfortune or disaster, regardless of the people's attitude toward Islam.

KHUMUS

One-fifth of the booty of war—khumus—must be surrendered to the Islamic State treasury as ordered by the Islamic Holy Constitution which also instructs the Islamic State how to spend such money or property.

> [Muslims must] know that whatever booty has come under your hand, one-fifth (khumus) of it has to be given to God and his Prophet [that is, the State of Islam], to [the Prophet's] relatives, the orphans, the needy, and the needy travellers, if you are believing in God and what we have sent down [revealed] upon our servant on the distinctive day; the day in which the two communities [the Muslims and non-Muslims] have met. And God is Omnipotent.
>
> *The Qur'ān* 8:41

Under Islam booty of war means only the property found on the battle field, including the headquarters of the enemy's army. The property of individuals who are not fighting is not considered booty and has been forbidden to be taken. However, all kinds of arms and weapons must be surrendered to the Islamic State and must not be divided among Muslim fighters.

LANDS

All lands that have not been legally claimed by individuals in the territorial jurisdiction of the Islamic State are state lands or national property. However, the Islamic Holy Constitution has established a provision for Muslims who may own such land even without the permission of the Islamic State. It has been stated by the Prophet that 'Whosoever activates [State] land it becomes his own' (Al-Bukhārī, *Ḥarth* 15; Ibn Ḥanbal, 1969, Vol. 3, pp. 303–4). Activation of land usually means the cultivation of land, which encourages rich Muslims to participate physically in national economic productivity.

ZAKĀH—TAXATION

Taxes in Islam are a religious duty, levied so that rich people may participate in helping the State provide for, and contribute toward furnishing a good living for the needy. Islam, by ordering the rich to pay their zakāh to the state directly, gives an excellent example of the humane vision of its regulations. By making the state responsible for the distribution of taxes to the needy, Islam has eliminated all sorts of humiliation that may be felt by the poor. The Islamic Holy Constitution considers such assistance to the poor and needy to be a task of the Islamic State and the poor, in turn, to have the right to be taken care of by the State. The Islamic Holy Constitution, moreover, prescribes outlets for the Islamic State to spend this taxation, as stated below:

> Charities are only for the poor, the needy, the collector of them, those who may be intimate [to Islam and/or Īmān], those who are captivated [to pay ransoms for them], the creditors [who bail or pay for reconcilation], the cause of God, and the needy traveller; [this is] the statute of God. God is Omniscient and Wise.
>
> *The Qur'ān* 9:60

Thus, a large portion of the Islamic Nation would benefit from zakāh. However, the term 'charity' has been used in this verse of the Islamic Holy Constitution to indicate that not only zakāh must be collected and given to those mentioned in the verse, but also other optional charities might be collected by the Islamic State at irregular intervals. Moreover, the cause of God mentioned in the verse as an outlet of charity is a broad category. It may include defense purposes as well as other services of the state for public welfare, such as schools, roads and health facilities.

Zakāh is levied on Muslims who are citizens of the Islamic State as an annual payment of surplus money or estates. In general, the tax payment is a sum of 2.5 percent of all money or estates that are superfluous to the Muslim's personal and family needs. These unused properties have to be in the Muslim's possession for a complete year. Their value must be equal to 624 gm of silver (3.12 gm × 200 dirham) or 93.69 gm of gold (4.68 gm × 20 miskal). Regarding livestock, such as camels, cows, goats and sheep, a certain amount has to be paid in money or kind when the animals reach the specified minimum and have been owned for one year. (For more details about the specified minimum of each of the animals, consult Ibn Qudāmah, 1956, Vol. 2, pp. 421–61, Vol. 3, pp. 35–58). Also all land products have to be taxed if they are almost equal to 840 kg., or their prices reach the specified minimum of that of silver or gold. The tax for land products are one-tenth of the naturally watered produce, one-fifteenth of half naturally watered and half artificially watered produce, and one-twentieth of completely artificially watered produce (Ibn Qudāmah, 1956, Vol. 3, pp. 1–34).

In respect to non-Muslim working men who are permanent residents of the Islamic State, they have to pay a maximum of 5 percent of their annual income in tax. This tax, collected from non-Muslims, is for providing protection and safety and for using such free public services as schools and health facilities. It is also in payment for their exemption from conscription. Cultivated land owned by those permanent residents also has to be taxed. The tax due ranges from 25 to 50 percent of the produce. At any rate, the Islamic State Supreme Court has to study the permanent residents' situation and decide, according to the practice of the Prophet and his four Right-guided Caliphs, the percentage of their income and land tax. It should be obvious that income and land taxes cannot both be levied on one person; either is enough and whichever is the higher should be collected.

'USHŪRE—CUSTOMS DUTY OR TARIFF

This kind of state income was introduced in the time of the second Caliph, 'Umar, when Muslim merchants complained that foreign countries charged duty on their goods. 'Umar, thus, ordered that the Islamic State at the time should act accordingly (Ibn Ādam, 1927, p. 173; Abū Yūsuf, 1952, pp. 69–78; Abū 'Ubaydah, 1933, p. 534). However, as there is no applicable text of the Islamic Holy Constitution, tariffs should be charged in accordance with foreign countries' treatment of the Islamic State. The Islamic State, however, can increase or decrease the tariff of any product depending on consumption and whether local production needs to be encouraged. Moreover, within the Islamic State each province can impose a certain percentage of tariff on its products to improve and encourage local government services.

INTESTATE ESTATES

The estate of any deceased citizen or permanent resident of the Islamic State who has no heirs and dies intestate reverts to the Islamic State.

In summary, Islam has provided the Islamic Nation with detailed laws governing the economic system and the national income of the State. In respect of the economy, Islamic regulations are founded on the ideas of justice and equality for all people without discrimination. Islam realized the difficulties and dangers of the accumulation of wealth, so it set up rational positive and prohibitive measures to assure the objectivity of its laws. The main objectives of these measures are twofold: to ease the lives of the unfortunate and to eliminate the concentration of wealth in the hands of a few Muslims.

Islam also provides a constant income for the state system. This regulation is designed to assure that Islam is not merely a religion practised only in places of worship, but also a complete system of life. It is deeply concerned with the welfare of human beings since it places the burden of providing a living for those who cannot afford it upon the state and not upon other human beings like them. This treatment is ordered to free the recipients from any submission to people, while always submitting to God.

Conclusion

'The Arab world is hard to govern', Hudson began the conclusion to his impressive work on the political culture of the contemporary Arab states, *Arab Politics, the Search for Legitimacy*. It is a sincere and truthful conceptualization of the Arabs' case, not only of the modern era but also of the centuries before the Islamic message was reveaed. Arabs are similar to their camels, in that they can never be ruled by an irrational system or by force. If the political system is basically irrational, Arabs will sooner or later rebel against it. The history of the Arab before Islam is one of continuous war and fighting with others and among themselves. The Arab personality and characteristic individuality will never be subdued by force or by haphazard policies.

The Arabs have found in Islam the system that suits their nature. 'No Sovereign except God' is the translation of the first word of entering the gate of Islam—*shahādah*. Islam has incorporated the political and social system which the Bedouin Muslims used to develop their civilization. The main components are structural and ideological legitimacy, with the necessary institutionalization of these ideologies and structures. Ideologies are an articulated set of ideals, ends and purposes which help the members of the system to interpret the past, explain the present and offer a vision for the future. (Easton 1965, p. 290).

The Islamic system has actually incorporated in its Holy Constitution a complete ideology. No scholar can deny the great effect Islam has upon the human character when it is sincerely held and vividly apprehended. Furthermore, Islamic ideology presents additional information about the unseen future of the world, and has drawn specific conclusions about certain aspects of universal and natural manifestations. At the same time, the Islamic system considers that dictatorial manipulations, which limit man's freedom, constitute one of the greatest sins directed against human beings and so must be eliminated from the earth by Muslims.

However, political structure is considered by modern political scientists to be an important source of legitimacy 'to constitute the framework within which 'accepted procedures' are carried out' (Hudson, 1977, p. 22). The Islamic Holy Constitution refers to the political structure as 'those who are in power amongst you' (*The Holy Qur'ān* 4:59). The Islamic political structure is completely devoid of manipulation. However, the governmental model of the Prophet in Medina and of ʿUmar, the second Right-guided Caliph, formally institutionalized the legitimacy of both the ideology and political structure of the early Islamic State. Of course, we do not emphasize that particular structure, but the methods by which organizations and procedures acquire value and stability. For this reason, too, the Islamic Holy Constitution does not discuss in detail the political structure of its system. However, the emphasis is always on the methods, processes and the framework which grant legitimacy to the system. To prescribe (how to do) is, in fact, more rational and legal than to designate (who is). Moreover, when describing the political structure of its system, the Islamic Holy Constitution always considers the nation or the state the legal agent rather than the individual. The major point behind the collective orientation is to create in the masses an interest in the political system with which they have identified themselves, their values and their individual and collective goals. By addressing the believers, the Islamic Holy Constitution encourages the Islamic Nation to castigate the politicians who may deviate from the prescribed provisions and goals of the system to serve their own interests.

Undoubtedly, most of the remaining Companions of the Prophet, after the fourth Right-guided Caliph was killed, realized that Muʿāwiyah and the whole Umayyad dynasty were illegitimate rulers, a fact that Muʿāwiyah and his successors also knew. The Umayyad rulers directed Muslims to the most important mission of the Islamic Nation, jihād or the call to Islam, in order to turn the attention of the Islamic Nation away from the legitimacy of the ruling class. Muʿāwiyah and his successors had started to prick the Arab's most sensitive spot, their racial chauvinism. Through gradual but highly developed political manipulation by both the Umayyad and Abbasid dynasties, Muslims started to forget the basic tenet of their faith which considers all people to be created equal out of dust and that no race or person should be superior to another. The Islamic Nation, after ʿAli was killed, lacked a strong leader to preserve it from illegitimate rulers. However, the religious community was fully responsible for the illegitimate political regime, since they either supported the ruling class or avoided them by dedicating their lives to teaching the Islamic Holy Constitution and Constitutional Law.

Finally, Islam is not, by any means, merely a religion or a personal code to be practised individually and in the mosques. Islam is rather a complete, systematic theology concerned with all aspects of Muslims' lives—political, social and religious. One of the most significant aspects of the Islamic System is its dynamic ability to change according to the prevailing circumstances of the time and place. This mechanism of change has, in effect, coloured all its provisions. Those provisions which are not subject to change or development can be temporarily replaced under severe or unexpected conditions. So any such slogan as Arabism, Nationalism or Socialism that the Arabs now hold is directed against their own faith and they will never be united in one nation unless they recognize that all Muslims, whatever the differences of race or colour, are one Nation which has to be united under the word of Islam.

Appendix: The Declaration of Medina

Rules Concerning the Citizens of the Islamic State

1. This is a Declaration (kitāb) of Muḥammad the Messenger of God [issued in his capacity as the leader of the first Islamic Nation] to operate amongst the faithful [Mu'minūm] and the submissive to God [Muslimūn] from amongst the Quraysh and the people of Yathrib [another name for Medina] and those who may follow and join them in jihād; verily they constitute one nation [that is, one political unit, *ummah* distinct from all other peoples [of the world].
2. The emigrants from amongst the Quraysh shall be responsible for the security of their quarter or ward (rabʿah) [concerning any crime occurring inside their quarter, of which the perpetrator is unknown or unable to pay the required sum for wergild, etc.]. They shall pay in mutual collaboration [that is, from their emergency insurance fund which exists in each tribe or its branch, which either annually or quarterly collects a certain amount from each individual related to the tribe by genealogy or by terms of partisanship (mawlā) to ensure the payment of any accident] the required payment [according to the law]. They are also responsible for ransom any of their captives, applying the principles of recognized goodness and justice amongst the believers.[1]

See Hamidullah, 1969 pp. 39–47. Before introducing the Arabic text of this declaration, Professor Hamidullah refers to references to the text in the languages into which it was translated. *See also* his own translation in his *The First Written Constitution in the World*, 1975, pp. 41–54.

1. The role of the police force may lessen such responsibility of the quarters' inhabitants; however, it should not completely vanish. Also the Islamic state may participate in the payment of wergild or ransom.

3. And the Banū ʿAwf [this and the following names are tribes or branches of the Anṣār] shall be responsible for the security of their quarter. They shall pay, in mutual collaboration, the required payment in accordance with their own established fashion of division and estimation of the wergild;[2] each division shall ransom its captive, applying the principles of recognized goodness and justice amongst the believers.
4. The Banū al-Hārith ibn al-Khazraj shall be responsible for the security of their quarter. They shall pay, in mutual collaboration, the required payment in accordance with their own established fashion of division and estimation of the wergild; each division shall ransom its captive, applying the principles of recognized goodness and justice amongst the believers.
5. The Banū Sāʿidah shall be responsible for the security of their quarter. They shall pay, in mutual collaboration the required payment in accordance with their own established fashion of division and estimation of the wergild; each division shall ransom its captive, applying the principles of recognized goodness and justice amongst the believers.
6. The Banū Jushm shall be responsible for the security of their quarter. They shall pay, in mutual collaboration the required payment according to their own established fashion of division and estimation of the wergild; each division shall ransom its captive, applying the principles of recognized goodness and justice amongst the believers.
7. The Banū al-Najjār shall be responsible for the security of their quarter. They shall pay, in mutual collaboration the required payment according to their own established fashion of division and estimation of the wergild; each division shall ransom its captive applying the principles of recognized goodness and justice amongst the believers.
8. The Banū ʿAmr ibn ʿAwf shall be responsible for the security of their quarter. They shall pay, in mutual collaboration, the required payment according to their own established fashion of division and estimation of the wergild; each division shall ransom its captive, applying the principles of recognized goodness and justice amongst the believers.

2. The estimation of wergild or injury was left temporarily as it was practised; after that everything was established according to the Islamic Holy Constitution's provisions in such matters.

9. The Banū al-Nabīṭ shall be responsible for the security of their quarter. They shall pay, in mutual collaboration the required payment according to their own established fashion of division and estimation of wergild; each division shall ransom its captive, applying the principles of recognized goodness and justice amongst the believers.
10. The Banū al-'Aws shall be responsible for the security of their quarter. They shall pay, in mutual collaboration the required payment in accordance with their own established fashion of division and estimation of the wergild; each division shall ransom its captive applying the principles of recognized goodness and justice amongst the believers.
11. The believers shall never leave any poor person suffering because he has no relative to pay for him the wergild or ransom. The believer shall provide, collectively, help for him in accordance with the principles of recognized goodness and justice.
12. The believer shall never become involved in an alliance with a person who is already an ally of another believer, either on the basis of tribe or branch of tribe.
13. Verily, the pious believers are collectively responsible for introducing to the due process of law any one of them who commits outrage, becomes iniquitous, commits a sin or aggression, or tries to undermine the good relations amongst the believers, even though he is a son of any one of them.
14. A believer shall not kill another believer in retaliation for a non-believer. Also a believer shall not help a non-believer against a believer, [without due process of law in any case].

Rules Concerning Peace and War

15. The Covenant of God is certainly an unchangeable one. So any believer who extends his own protection to any one, [to prevent him from any iniquituous act] all the believers shall be obliged to carry out such protection. Therefore, the believers are obligated towards each other [in terms of justice and equality] against all other peoples.
16. Those who are [or will be] residents within the jurisdiction of the Islamic State from amongst the Jews shall be protected by

the believers equally without any prejudice, nor shall any kind of help be extended to their enemies against them.

17. In any fighting in the cause of God, a treaty of peace must be extended to cover all the believers. Consequently, a believer must never conclude a peace treaty for himself alone with the non-believer. Such a treaty must include all the believers in terms of equality and justice for all of them.
18. The armed forces of the Islamic State shall participate in the fighting in the cause of God by turn without discrimination.
19. The believers as a unit shall defend each other and take the responsibility of fighting for each other in any battle in the cause of God.
20. The pious believers shall always be the followers of the best and straight guidance [in terms of justice and equitableness].
21. Any polytheist who may extend his protection to property or life of the Quraysh will be considered against the believers, as those who prevent the extension of protection to a believer will be considered also against the believers.
22. Any one who intentionally kills a believer, and his act is legally proven, he shall be killed unless the heirs of the murdered person agree to extend their forgiveness and except the wer-gild. The believers must be, collectively, responsible for the performance of due process of law in such matter.
23. It is proscribed as illegal for all the believers, who admit the legality of this Declaration as they admit their belief in God and the Last Day, to help any criminal or protect him against the due process of law. So whosoever extends his help or protection to such a person, verily God's curse and wrath shall be on him in the Last Day, in which he will not find any protectors nor will any excuse be accepted for him.
24. Whatever dispute arises concerning any legal matter, it must be then referred to God and to Muḥammad, [i.e., the Islamic Holy Constitution and the authority of the Islamic State].

Rules Concerning the Non-Muslim Residents

25. The Jews shall be responsible for their own expenditures as long as the fighting is against them.
26. And, the Jews of the Banū ʿAwf shall be considered a community

(ummah)—themselves and their partisans—along with the believers. For the Jews their religion and for the believers their religion, with the exception that anyone of the Jews who commits a heinous crime or sin will be liquidating himself and his family.

27. And the Jews of Banū al-Najjār shall be treated like those of the Banū ʿAwf.
28. And the Jews of the Banū al-Hārith shall be treated like those of the Banū ʿAwf.
29. And the Jews of the Banū Sāʾidah shall be treated like those of the Banū ʿAwf.
30. And the Jews of the Banū Jushm shall be treated like those of the Banū ʿAwf.
31. And the Jews of the Banū al-ʾAws shall be treated like those of the Banū ʿAwf.
32. And the Jews of the Banū Thaʿlabah shall be treated like those of the Banū ʿAwf, wth the exception of any one who commits an heinous crime or sin will be liquidating himself and his family.
33. And the Jews of Jafnah is a branch of the Thaʿlabah as themselves.
34. And the Jews of the Banū al-Shuṭibiyyah shall be treated like those of the Banū ʿAwf. Certainly goodness is better than sin.
35. And, the partisans of the Thaʿlabah shall be as the Thaʿlabah themselves.
36. And the friend of the Jews will be treated as the Jews themselves.
37. None of these Jews will leave the territorial jurisdiction of the Islamic State without the permission of Muḥammad [that is the authority of the Islamic State].
38. The due process of law must be carried out for any criminal act, there shall be no right for anyone to prevent the law to be carried out by the Islamic State. Therefore, anyone who commits a crime, will be completely responsible, he and his family [to introduce him to the authority]; otherwise, to prevent the due process of law will be considered an action against the state. God is certainly with those who observe His law.
39. Certainly the Jews will be responsible for their outlay as the believers also will be responsible for their outlay. The believers as well as the Jews have to help each other against any party

that intends to fight those who have been mentioned in this Declaration, both the believers and the Jews have to advise each other of goodness and to prevent sin.

40. None can be held guilty for whatever his ally has done. Certainly help shall be provided for anyone who has been tyrannized.
41. The Jews will be responsible concerning their expenditure as long as the fighting is against them.
42. Verily, Yathrib shall constitute inviolable Islamic territory for the parties mentioned in this Declaration.
43. The protected person shall be treated as the protector himself without prejudice or injustice.
44. No protection shall be extended by the protected person without the permission of the original protector.
45. Any kind of crime or dispute which may result in disunity between those mentioned in this Declaration must be referred to God and Muḥammad the Messenger of God [that is, the Islamic Holy Constitution and the Islamic State authority] God certainly will guarantee the protection and guidance of those who observe the rules of this Declaration.
46. No protection shall be given to the Quraysh and their allies [by those mentioned in this Declaration].
47. Extensive help must be provided by all parties mentioned in this Declaration against any attack or invasion of Yathrib.
48. If the believers call for any sort of conciliation or peace, the non-believers have to participate and adhere to it; and if the non-believers call for such, likewise the believers have to participate and adhere to it with the exception of fighting against the religion of Islam.
49. Then, each party has to carry out their responsibility for the security and participation in defence and keeping order of their quarter.
50. And the Jews of al-ʾAws themselves and their partisans shall be responsible equally as those parties mentioned in this Declaration with pure sincerity and good intention of all parties therewith. Goodness is better than sin; evil-doers are working against themselves alone. Verily God is with the truthful one who observes the rules in this Declaration.
51. The contents of this Declaration do not relieve any sinner or iniquitous person of legal punishment.

52. Anyone who leaves or stays in Medina must be secured properly, with the exception of a sinner or an iniquitous person.
53. God is the protector of anyone who observes goodness and piety. Muḥammad the Messenger of God [is the witness].

Select Bibliography

Arabic References

The Holy Qur'ān.

Ibn Adam, Yaḥyab, *Kitāb al-Kharāj*. Cairo: Al-Maktabah al-Salafiyyah, 1927.

Al-'Asbahī, Mālik ibn Anas, *Al-Muwaṭṭā'*. Ed., M. F. Abd al-Baqi. Cairo: Al-Halbai, 1951, 2 vols.

Al-Ashʿarī, ʿAli, E., *Maqālāt al-Islāmiyyīn*. Ed., M. M. Abd al-Hamīd. Cairo: Al-Nahdah al-Massriyyah, 1969.

Al-Bāqillānī, Abū Bakr M., *Al-Tamhīd*. Beirut: Dar al-Taliʿah, 1947.

Al-Bukhārī, Muḥammad ibn Ismāʿil, *Al-Jāmiʿ al-Ṣaḥiḥ*. Ed., Muḥammad F. Abd al-Bāqī. Cairo: Al-Salafiyah Press, 1961, 4 vols.

Al-Dārimī, Abdullah ibn Abdalrahman, *Sunan al-Dārimī*. Cairo: Īḥya' al-Sunnah Press, n.d., 2 vols.

Abū-Dāwūd, Sulaimān ibn al-ashʿth al-Sajestānī al-Azdi, *Sunan Abī Dāwūd* or *Kitab al-Sunan*. Ed., Muḥammad M. Abdal-Hamid. Cairo: Iḥyā' al-Sunnah Press, n.d., 4 vols.

Ḥamidullah, Muḥammad, *Al-Watha'iq al-Siyāsiyyah*. Beirute: Dar al-Irshad, 1969, 3rd Ed.

Ibn Ḥanbal-Aḥmed ibn Muḥammad al-Shaybānī, *Al-Musnad*. Beirute: Islamic Office, 1969, 6 vols.

Ibn-Hishām, Abdulmalik ibn Hishām al-Maʿafrī, *Al-Sīrah al-Nabawiyyah*. Ed., Mustafā al-Saggā. Cairo: Al-Halabi, 1955, 2nd Ed., 2 vols.

Ḥusayn, M. M., *Al-Ittijāhāt al-Waṭaniyyah Fi al-Adab al-Muʿāsir*. Cairo: Al-Adāb Library, 1954.

Ibish, Yūsaf, *Nuṣūṣ al-Fikr al-Siyasi al-Islāmī*. Beirut: Dar al-Taliʿah, 1966.

Al-Kattānī, abd al-Ḥay, *Nizām al-Ḥukūmah al-Nabawiyyah*. Beirut: Ihya' al-Trāth al-Arabī, n.d.

Kurdī, Abd al-Rahmān, A., *Scientific Methods Used to Authenticate the Prophet's Sunnah: A comparative Study With the Historian's Method.* Unpublished master's thesis, Umm-al-Qurā University, Makkah 1974.

Ibn Mājah, Abū Abdallah Muḥammad ibn Yazid al-Qazwīnī, *Sunan ibn Mājah.* Cairo: Al-Halabi, n.d., 2 vols.

Ibn Manẓūr, Muḥammad ibn Mukarram al-Anṣarī, *Lisan al-Arab.* Cairo: Al-Masriyyah Li al-Nasher, n.d., 9 vols.

Al-Māwardī, ʿAlī M., *Adb al-Qāḍī.* Ed., M. H. Al-Sarḥan. Baghdad: Irshad Press, 1971.

Al-Māwardī, ʿAlī M., *Al-Aḥkam al-Sulṭāniyyah.* Cairo: Al-Halabi, 1966.

Muslim, Muslim ibn al-Hajāj, *Ṣaḥiḥ Muslim.* Ed., N. F. Abd al-Baqi. Cairo: Dar al-Turath al-Arabī 1956.

Al-Nasāʾī, Aḥmed ibn Shuʿib ibn ʿAlī, *Al-Mujtabā or Sunan al-Nisāʾi.* Cairo: Al-Halabi, 1964, 8 vols.

Ibn al-Qayyim, M. A., *Eʿlām al-Muwaqqʿīn.* Ed., Ṭaha A. Saʿad. Cairo: Azhar Colleges Library, 1968.

Ibn Qudāmah, Abdulla, *Al-Mughnī.* Ed., Ṭaha M. al-Zzyni. Cairo: Cairo Library, 1956.

Al-Qurṭubī, M. ibn Faraj, *Aqḍiyat Rasūl-Allah.* Aleppo, Syria: Dar al-Wa i, 1976.

Al-Ṭabarī, Muḥammad ibn Jarīr, *Tarikh al-Rusul wa al-Mulūk.* Ed., M. A. Ibrahim. Cairo: Dar al-Maʿārif, 1962.

Al-Ṭabarī, Muḥammad ibn Jarīr, *Jamʿ al-Bayān ʿAn Taʾwīl Ayī al-Qurʾān.* Cairo: Al-Halabi, 1968.

Al-Tirmidhī, Muḥāmmad ibn ʿIsa ibn Sawarah, *Al-Jamiʿ al-Ṣaḥiḥ or Sunan al-Tirmidhī.* Ed., Ahmed M. Shaker. Cairo: Al-Halabi Press, 1937, 4 vols.

Abū ʿUbaydah, Al-Qasim ibn Sallām, *Al-Amwāl.* Ed., M.H. Al-Faqī. Cairo: Al-Maktaba al-Salafiyyah, 1933.

Abū Yūsuf, Yaʿqūb I., *Kitāb al-Kharāj.* Cairo: Al-Maktuba al-Salafiyyah, 1952.

Zallum, Abd al-Qadim, *Kayfa Hudimat al-Khilāfah.* No location: no publisher available, 1962.

English References

Abraham, Henry J., *The Judicial Process: An Introductory Analysis of the Courts of the United States, England, and France.* New York: Oxford University Press, 1980.

Arnold, T. W., *The Preaching of Islam*. London: Constable, 1935, 3rd Ed.

Bailey, Frank Edgar, *British Policy and Turkish Reform Movement: A Study in Anglo-Turkish Relation (1826–1853)*. Cambridge: Harvard University Press, 1942.

Bentham, Jeremy, *A Fragment on Government and an Introduction to the Principles of Morals and Legislation*. Ed., Wilfred Harrison. New York: Macmillan, 1948.

Blackstone, Sir William, *Commentaries on the Laws of England*. London: W. Strahan T. Cadell, 1783, 9th Ed.

Bodin, Jean, *Six Books of the Commonwealth*. Abridged and translated by M. J. Tooley. Oxford: Blackwell, 1967.

Brecht, Arnold, *Political Theory: The Foundations of Twentieth-Century Political Thought*. Princeton, New Jersey: Princeton University Press, 1959.

Crick, Bernard, 'Sovereignty', *International Encyclopedia of the Social Sciences*. New York: Macmillan, 1968.

Dar, Bashir Ahmed, *Qurʾānic Ethics*. Lahore: Institution of Islamic Culture, 1969.

Demaris, Ovid, *Dirty Business: The Corporate-Political Money-power Game*. New York: Harper's Magazine Press, 1974.

Dorfman, Joseph, *The Economic Mind in American Civilization*. New York: Viking Press, 1946.

Easton, David, *A System Analysis of Political Life*. New York: Wiley, 1965.

Gilson, Etiene, *Reason and Revelation in the Middle Ages*. New York: Wiley, 1939.

Ḥamidullah, Muḥammad, *The First Written Constitution in the World*. Lahore: Muhammad Ashraf, 1975, 3rd Ed.

Hamilton, Alexander, *The Federalist, a Commentary on the Constitution of the United States*. Ed., Henry Cabot Lodge. New York: G. P. Putman's Sons, 1895.

Hayes, Calton J. H., *Essays on Nationalism*. New York: Macmillan, 1937.

Hobbes, Thomas, *Leviathan*. Reprint of 1651 Edition with an essay by the late W. G. Pogson Smith. Oxford: The Clarendon Press, 1965.

Hudson, Michael C., *Arab Politics: The Search for Legitimacy*. New Haven: Yale University Press, 1977.

Iqbāl, Muḥammad, *The Reconstruction of the Religious Thought in Islam*. Lahore: Muḥammad Ashraf, 1950.

Kant, Immanuel, *Critque of Pure Reason*. Tr., J. M. D. Meiklejohn. New York: P. F. Collier & Son, 1900.

Kern, Fritz, *Kingship and Law in the Middle Ages*. Tr., S. B. Chrines. Oxford: University Press, 1939.

Kohn, Hans, *The Idea of Nationalism*. New York: Macmillan, 1944.

Oppenheim, Felix E., *Dimensions of Freedom; An Analysis*. New York: St. Martins Press, 1961.

Parekh, Bhikin, *Jeremy Bentham: Political Thought*. Ed., Bhikhu Parekh. London: Croom Helm, 1973.

Phillips, Keniv P, and Paul H. Blackman, *Electoral Reform and* Voter *Participation*. Washington, D.C.: American Enterprise Institute, 1975.

Popkin, Richard H. and Avrum Stroll, *Philosophy Made Easy*. New York: Holt, Rinehart and Winston, 1956.

Rietman, Alan and Robert B. Davidson, *The Election Process, Voting Laws and Procedures*. Dobbs Ferry, New York: Oceana, 1972.

Rosenthal, Erwin I. J., *Political Thought in Medieval Islam*. Cambridge: The University Press, 1962.

Rosenthal, Erwin I. J., *Islam in the Modern National State*. Cambridge: The University Press, 1965.

Russell, Bertrand, 'Freedom and Government', in Ruth N. Anshen, Ed., *Freedom Its Meaning*. New York: Macmillan, 1941.

Schacht, Joseph, *The Origins of Muḥammadan Jurisprudence*. Oxford: The Clarendon Press, 1950.

Smith, Colin L., *The Embassy of Sir William White at Constantinople 1886–1891*. Westport, Conn.: Greenwood Press, 1979.

Smith, C. Ryder, 'Theocracy', *Encyclopedia of Religion and Ethics*. New York: Charles Scribner's Sons, 1924.

Thompson, Dennis F., *The Democratic Citizen: Social Science and Democratic Theory in the Twentieth Century*. Cambridge: The University Press, 1970.

Wellhausen, Julius, *The Arab Kingdom and its Fall*. Tr., Margaret Graham·Wier. Calcutta: Calcutta University Press, 1927.

Wensnick, A.J. and J. Burgman, *Concordance et Indices de la Tradition Musulmane*. Leiden: E. J. Brill 1936–69.

Wilkerson, T. E., *Kant's Critique of Pure Reason: A Commentary for Students*. Oxford: Clarendon Press, 1976.

Index

Abbāsid dynasty 3, 128
ʿAbduh, Muḥammed 11
administration, control of 78–9
alcohol, proscription of 29–30
ʿAli 128
aliens, *see* non-Muslims
analogy, logical (qiyās) 12, 89
apostasy, law of 52–3, 58
Arabic language 4, 5, 13, 23, 80, 88–9
 contemporary usage 9–10, 103–4
 and nationality 53–4, 56
armies, Islamic 59, 66, 91, 103, 110, 134
Asad, Muḥammad 11
ʾAshʿarite theologians 36
Abū Bakr 15, 63, 70–1, 110
Al-Bāqillānī 15

Bentham, Jeremy 36
Blackstone, Sir William 36
Bodin, Jean 36
booty (khumus) 110, 121–2
Brecht, Arnold 42
business function of state 68

cabinet 78, 93, 94
Caliphs, four Right-guided 11, 13, 38, 63, 66, 70–1, 77, 90, 110, 124, 128
 and Islamic law 85
Cassation Court 88, 89
charity 47, 48, 116, 120, 123
Chief Justice 79, 92–3, 95
Commitment Oath 75–6, 81
Companions of the Prophet 54, 90
 and Islamic law 3–4, 12–13, 45–6, 78, 85, 86
competition, economic 68, 117–18
Congress, Islamic 9, 38, 72, 78–9, 82–3, 92–3; *see also* legislature
conscription, law of 59, 101, 111, 124
Constituent Assembly 74, 78
Constitution, Islamic Holy 4–6, 7–9, 11–14, 15, 88–9, 94, 96, 127–8
 jihād in 100–4, 106–7
 ruling systems 16–25, 63, 128
 and superstructure laws 41
 and universality 41–2
 see also ethics; Law, Constitutional; reason; Revelation, Holy; sovereignty
Court, Islamic 59–60, 66–7, 79, 84–5; *see also* Supreme Court
Crick, Bernard 36–7
Criminal Court 88
customs duty (ʿushūre) 124

Declaration, Presidential 94
Declaration of Medina 15, 55, 58–9, 64, 94, 99, 131–7
defence, *see* jihād
democracy and Islam 7, 39, 63–4, 77, 118
Descartes, Rene 31–2
development, necessity for 1, 10, 41–2, 78, 96, 129
disputes, settlement of 85

economy 14, 113–25; *see also* hoarding; income, national; inheritance, law of; interest; monopoly; taxation; usury; wealth education for non-Muslims 60
election (shūrā) 38, 63, 69–77, 78, 82, 89, 95
  Presidential 92–3
enfranchisement 69, 72, 75
epistemology, *see* knowledge
equality, concept of 1, 14, 16, 19, 22, 25, 42–6, 61, 78, 96, 98, 113, 124, 128
  of opportunity 114
  and sovereignty 38, 64
ethics 16, 33–5, 47, 50; *see also* justice
executive 7–8, 83, 86, 90–6
  review of 86–7, 88, 90
  see also cabinet; election; head of state
exegesis, method of 13
expenditure, wasteful, ban on 120

faith (īmān) 3–4, 28, 47–50
foreign policy 91–2
foreign service, Islamic 67
freedom, right of 6, 16, 22, 42, 50–3, 64, 127–8
  in European tradition 50
  of faith 9, 28–9, 51–2, 60, 66, 98, 107–8

General Civil Court 88
Gilson, Etiene 27
governor, provincial 78, 95

Ḥadith 13
Hamidullah, Muḥammad 131n.
head of state 87
  authority 38, 96
  election of 72, 75–6, 78, 92–3
  responsibilities 7, 9, 15, 90–2, 94
  see also executive
history:
  heritage of 53–4, 56, 92
  interpretation of 2
hoarding (iddikhār), ban on 119–20
Hobbes, Thomas 36
Hudson, Michael C. 127, 128
Hume, David 32

Ibn ʿAffān, ʿUthām 71
Ibn ʿAwf, Abd al-Rḥaman 71
Ibn al-Khaṭṭāb, ʿUmar 71
income, national 121–5
  booty (khumus) 121–2
  customs duty (ʿushūre) 124
  intestate estates 124
  lands 122
  resources, natural 121
  see also wealth: national; taxation
income tax (jizyah) 59, 94; *see also* taxation
inheritance, law of 115–16
interest 118
Iqbāl, Muḥammad 3
Islam, definitions 2, 3–4

Abū Jandal 111
Jews 58, 133, 134–6; *see also* non-Muslims
jihad 100–9, 128, 131
  as call to Islam 108–9
  in defence of nation 66, 102–4
  as salvation and liberation 104–8
  see also war: lawful

judge, role of 49–50, 83–5, 87–9;
see also judiciary judgements, declaratory (al-Shurūṭ) 86
judiciary 7, 81, 83–90
functions of 83–7
judicial review 86–7
organization of 87–90
personnel 88–9
selection of 89
separation of 83
see also Chief Justice; judges
junta system (malā') 19–20, 23
jurisprudence, traditional schools of 10, 11
jurists (fuqahā') 2, 7, 10, 14, 74, 78, 79–83, 89–90, 92, 95
justice, concept of 1, 14, 16, 19, 22, 25, 42, 46–50, 61, 66, 78, 84, 96, 98, 113, 124
distributive 47
and faith 47–50
and sovereignty 38, 64

Kant, Immanuel 32
khalīfah (vice-gerent) 23–4
kharāj system 60
knowledge:
in Islam 26, 43–4, 102
philosophical theories of 31–2

Law, Constitutional (sharīʿah) 3, 6–12, 15, 77, 88, 102
as binding 9
interpretation of 6–8, 77–8
revision of 9–10
law, due process of 6, 44, 133, 134, 135
leadership, Islamic 17–18, 19, 37–9, 128–9; *see also* election; head of state
legislature 77–83, 94–5
constituent function 77–8
control of administration 78–9, 90–2
discipline 79
electoral function 78
representation 80–1
review of 87, 88
statue-making function 78, 86
structure 79–80
tenure of office 80
see also Congress, Islamic
Locke, John 32

man, Islamic view of 79–80, 97–8, 99
Al-Mawdūdī 11
monarchical system (mulk) 1, 17–19, 23, 63; *see also* sovereignty
monopoly, ban on 117–18
Mu ʿāwiyah 128
Muḥammad 63, 66, 70, 72, 77, 90, 105–6, 110–11
as example 9–11, 35, 54, 90, 96, 124, 128
and Islamic law 12–13, 15, 85
see also Declaration of Medina
Mu ʿtazilite theologians 36

Nation, Islamic 64–5, 131
degeneration of 1–2, 55–6
rights and duties of 69–77
and sovereignty 37–9, 63
see also nationality, Muslim; State, Islamic
National Guard (muriābiṭūn) 101–2, 111–12
nationalism 2, 53, 55–6, 129
nationality, Muslim 42, 53–7, 61
non-Muslims, status of 9, 42, 45, 57–61, 134–7
as enemies 103–4, 108–9

obedience (bayʿah) 69, 71, 75–6, 96

peace, concept of 14, 97, 98, 100, 111–12, 133–4
Personal Statute Court 88

police force, Islamic 66
politics, party, ban on 73
power, *see* sovereignty
President, *see* executive; head of state
professionals in legislature 74, 78–83, 92, 95
public office 59, 72–5, 78

Qur'ān 2, 4–5, 12, 80, 92, 104–7
on charity 120, 123
on equality 43–4, 72
on ethics 35
on freedom 51–2, 66
on hoarding 119
on individual and state 65
on inheritance 115–16
on justice 48–9, 85
on law 8
on nationality 54, 56–7
on non-Muslims 57–8, 97
on obedience 76
on reason/revelation 25–31
on role of women 72
on ruling systems 16–24
on sovereignty 37–9, 69
on usury 118
on war 99–103, 107–8, 111
on wasteful expenditure 120
on wealth 114–15
on welfare services 67

reason:
and ethics 34
and revelation 16, 18, 25–32
'Record of Legal Cases' (Kitāb al-Aqḍiyah) 84–5
Revelation, Holy 3–4; *see also* Constitution; reason; Qur'ān; Sunnah
Riḍā, Rashūd 11
rights, human 60–1, 100; *see also* equality; freedom; justice
Rosenthal, Erwin I.J. 2
Russell, Bertrand 50

scientists, religious ('ulama') 2
sectarianism, religious 2, 9–10
service functions of state 59, 67–8, 94, 95–6, 121, 122–3
Services, Divine 1, 6, 9, 41, 94, 100
Shahādah 76, 127
shūrā, *see* election
sovereignty 16, 35–9, 103
of God 3, 36–7, 76, 104–5, 127
State, Islamic:
function of 65–8
and the individual 64–5, 68
organization of 63–4, 69–96
purpose of 64–5
theory of 11, 12
statutes, personal 1, 41, 94
Sufism 80
Summary Court 88
Sunnah 2, 4–5, 12, 80, 92, 106–7
on equality 45–6
on ethics 34
on inheritance 116
on justice 47, 50, 84
on law 8
on monopoly 117–18
on nationality 54
on natural resources 121
on non-Muslims 45, 97
on political office 73–5
on role of women 72
on ruling systems 16
on war 103, 108, 109–11
on wealth 113
on welfare services 67–8
Supreme Court, Islamic 7, 74, 77–9, 81–2, 86–7, 88–9, 92–5, 116, 124
membership of 89–90

Al-Ṭabarī, Muḥammad ibn Jarir 71
tax system (zakah) 6, 60, 67, 74, 117, 119, 122–4; *see also* income tax

tyrannical system (tāghūt) 21–2, 127–8

Abū ʿUbaydah, Al-Qasim ibn Saltam 9, 70
ʿUmar 70–1, 84, 86, 124, 128
Umayyad dynasty 128
universality of Islam 106
usury (ribā), ban on 118–19

Vice President 78, 92–3; *see also* executive

wage level, determination of 68
war, concept of 14, 91, 97–100
  declaration of 95
  lawful (jihād) 99, 100–9, 111
  rules of 109–12, 133–4
  unlawful 98–100
wealth:
  distribution of 114–16, 117, 124–5
  national 114–15, 121–5
  personal 113, 114–15, 116–18, 119–20
wergild (ransom) 55, 131–3, 134
women, role of 72
wrongful acts, prevention of 85–6